ADVANCES IN DIGITAL HANDWRITTEN SIGNATURE PROCESSING
A Human Artefact for e-Society

ADVANCES IN DIGITAL HANDWRITTEN SIGNATURE PROCESSING
A Human Artefact for e-Society

edited by

Giuseppe Pirlo
Università di Bari, Italy

Donato Impedovo
Politecnico di Bari, Italy

Michael Fairhurst
University of Kent, UK

World Scientific

NEW JERSEY · LONDON · SINGAPORE · BEIJING · SHANGHAI · HONG KONG · TAIPEI · CHENNAI

Published by

World Scientific Publishing Co. Pte. Ltd.
5 Toh Tuck Link, Singapore 596224
USA office: 27 Warren Street, Suite 401-402, Hackensack, NJ 07601
UK office: 57 Shelton Street, Covent Garden, London WC2H 9HE

Library of Congress Cataloging-in-Publication Data
Advances in digital handwritten signature processing : a human artefact for e-society / edited by
Giuseppe Pirlo (Università di Bari, Italy), Donato Impedovo (Politecnico di Bari, Italy), &
Michael Fairhurst (University of Kent, UK).
     pages cm
   Includes bibliographical references and index.
   ISBN 978-9814579629 (hardcover : alk. paper)
   1. Optical character recognition. 2. Digital signatures. I. Pirlo, Giuseppe, editor of compilation.
II. Impedovo, Donato, editor of compilation. III. Fairhurst, Michael C., 1948– editor of
compilation.
   TA1640.A278 2014
   006.4'24--dc23
                                                                 2014007538

British Library Cataloguing-in-Publication Data
A catalogue record for this book is available from the British Library.

Printed in Singapore

Preface

This book contains the enhanced versions of selected papers presented at the International Workshop on Emerging Aspects in Handwritten Signature Processing, held in Naples (Italy), September 9, 2013. The papers concerns a wide range of scientific issues related to online and offline handwritten signature processing but also highlights some relevant aspects related to the applications of handwritten signature in commercial systems, providing advanced solutions for the development of the Digital Agenda.

In particular, the paper "Stability Analysis of Online Signatures in the Generation Domain", by Giuseppe Pirlo, Donato Impedovo, Rejean Plamondon and Christian O'Reilly presents a new approach for the analysis of local stability in online signature. Conversely to previous approaches in the literature, in this case the analysis of stability is performed considering the strokes underlying the signing process and defined according to the Sigma-Lognormal model.

The paper "Exploiting Stability Regions for Online Signature Verification", by Antonio Parziale and Angelo Marcelli presents a method for finding the stability regions within a set of genuine signatures and for selecting the most suitable ones to be used for online signature verification. The definition of stability region builds upon motor learning and adaptation in handwriting generation, while their selection exploits both their ability to model signing habits and their effectiveness in capturing distinctive features.

The paper "Two Bioinspired Methods for Dynamic Signatures Analysis", by Jânio Canuto, Bernadette Dorizzi and Jugurta Montalvão focuses on the problem of dynamic signature segmentation and representation and proposes two dynamic signature segmentation/representation methods. Both methods are based on psychophysical evidences that led to the well-known Minimum Jerk principle and are good alternatives to the existing techniques.

In the paper "Using Global Features for Pre-Classification in Online Signature Verification Systems", by Marianela Parodi and Juan C. Gomez, a pre-classification stage based on global features is incorporated to an online signature verification system for the purposes of improving its performance. The pre-classifier makes use of some global features that are considered individually and in a combined form. The subsequent classification stage is based on features obtained from a wavelet approximation of the time functions associated with the signing process.

The paper "Instance Selection Method in Multi-Expert System for Online Signature Verification", by Giuseppe Pirlo, Donato Barbuzzi and Donato Impedovo, proposes a new feedback-based learning strategy to update the knowledge-base in multi-expert signature verification system. In this case, the collective behavior of classifiers is considered to select the samples for updating system knowledge.

The paper "Towards a Shared Conceptualization for Automatic Signature Verification", by Marcus Liwicki, Muhammad Imran Malik and Charles Berger, is an effort towards the development of a shared conceptualization regarding automatic signature verification especially between the Pattern Recognition (PR) and Forensic Handwriting Examiners (FHEs) communities. This is required because FHEs require state-of-the-art PR systems to incorporate them in forensic casework but so far most of these systems are not directly applicable to such environments. The paper, therefore, addresses three major areas where the two communities differ and suggest possible solutions to their effect.

The paper "Offline Signature Verification based on probabilistic Representation of Grid Events" by Konstantina Barkoula, Elias N. Zois, Evangelos Zervas and George Economou, presents a new grid based feature extraction methodology for offline handwritten signature representation. The approach mutates the informative content of a set of binary mask elements by considering them as probabilistic events, simple or compound.

The purpose of the paper "Local Features for Off-line Forensic Signature Verification", by Muhammad Imran Malik, Marcus

Liwicki and Andreas Dengel, is twofold. First, the authors debate on the importance of disguised signatures with examples in order to draw the attention of PR community this important genre of signatures. Second, they present a novel comparison among three local features based off-line systems for forensic signature verification. The first system is a combination of scale-invariant Speeded Up Robust Features (SURF) and Fast Retina Keypoints (FREAK). The second system is based on a combination of Features from Accelerated Segment Test (FAST) and FREAK and the third system is based on nine local features with Gaussian Mixture Models (GMMs) classification.

The paper "Emerging Issues for Static Handwritten Signature Biometrics", by Moises Diaz-Cabrera, Aythami Morales and Miguel A. Ferrer presents a review of the most recent advances in static/off-line signature recognition using Computer Vision. In addition, it also identifies some new trends and research opportunities such as the generation of synthetic signatures, time drifting, forger and disguise identification and multilingual scenarios.

The paper "Biometric Signatures in Mobility: the need for Transformation and the Opportunity for Innovation", by Emilio Paterlini, discusses how the growing demand for paperless processes in enterprise and government is pushing the development and widespread uptake of innovative technologies, with a strong focus on biometric signatures and new consumer devices.

The paper "Biometric Handwritten Solution: A World in a Signature", by Carlo Nava, presents some advances in the application of biometric signature. In particular, a biometric signature infrastructure is proposed in order to start the process of acquisition of the contracts that are concluded with the end customer in a "paperless" mode.

As Editors of this volume, we would like to thank all the authors for their valuable contributions and the members of the Scientific Committee for the accurate revision process. We want also thank the sponsors of this volume. In particular, as scientific association, the Italian Group of Pattern Recognition Researchers (GIRPR) and the International Graphonomic Society (IGS); as industrial companies, Accenture and Hewlett Packard.

Finally, we are grateful to the Amanda Yun, Editor of the World Scientific Publishing, for her kind and valued cooperation and suggestions in all phases of the publication of this issue.

The Editors
Giuseppe Pirlo
Donato Impedovo
Michael Fairhurst

Contents

SCIENTIFIC COMMITTEE

Marjory Abreu (Brazil)
Michael Blumenstein (Australia)
Bernadette Dorizzi (France)
Alexander Filatov (US)
Sonia Garcia-Salicetti (France)
Laurent Heutte (France)
Alexander Landau (US)
Marcus Liwicki (Germany)
Angelo Marcelli (Italy)
Javier Ortega-Garcia (Spain)
Umapada Pal (India)
Réjean Plamondon (Canada)
Robert Sabourin (Canada)
Christian Viard-Gaudin (France)
Claus Vielhauer (Germany)
Nicole Vincent (France)
Elias Zois (Greece)

SPONSORS

GIRPR - Gruppo Italiano Ricercatori in Pattern Recognition
(Italian Group Researchers in Pattern Recognition)

IGS – International Graphonomic Society

Accenture

Hewlett-Packard

CHAPTER 1

STABILITY ANALYSIS OF ONLINE SIGNATURES IN THE GENERATION DOMAIN

G. Pirlo[1], D. Impedovo[2], R. Plamondon[3], C. O'Reilly[3]

[1] *Dipartimento di Informatica, Università degli Studi di Bari, Italy*
{giuseppe.pirlo@uniba.it}

[2] *Dip. Meccanica, Matematica e Management, Politecnico di Bari, Italy*
{impedovo@deemail.poliba.it}

[3] *École Polytechnique de Montréal, Canada*
{rejean.plamondon, christian.oreilly}@polymtl.ca

This paper presents a new approach for the analysis of local stability in online signature. Conversely to previous approaches in the literature, the analysis of stability is here performed by considering the characteristics of the processes underlying signature generation. For this purpose, the Sigma-Lognormal model developed in the context of the kinematic theory of rapid human movements is considered. It allows the representation of the information of the neuromuscular system involved in the production of complex movements like signatures.

The experimental results were obtained using the SuSig database. They demonstrate that the new approach provides useful information on stability of online signatures and allows to better understand some characteristics of human behavior in signing.

1. Introduction

With the ubiquity of the internet in the modern society, the possibility to face actively social and economic transformations requires the development of new effective and efficient technologies and systems. Among others, the need for secure personal authentication is a crucial aspect in a multitude of applications related to the development of the Digital Agenda for e-health, e-government, e-justice, and so on.[1,2,3]

For this purpose, biometrics has been considered with a renewed interest in recent years. Biometrics refers to individual recognition based on a person's distinguishing characteristics. While other techniques use the possession of a token (i.e. badge, ID card, etc.) or the knowledge of something (i.e. a password, key phase, etc.) to perform personal recognition, biometric techniques offer the potential to use the inherent characteristics of the person to perform this task.[3]

Furthermore handwritten signature has a very special place in the wide set of biometric means that can be used for personal verification. Administrative and financial institutions recognize handwritten signatures as a legal means of verifying an individual's identity. In addition, people are familiar with the use of signatures in their daily life. Therefore, it is not surprising that a special interest has been recently devoted to the field of automatic signature verification.[4,5]

Unfortunately, a handwritten signature is a very complex trait. The rapid writing movement underlying handwritten signature generation is determined by a motor program stored into the signer's brain and implemented through the signer's writing system and writing devices (paper and pen type, etc.). Therefore, each handwritten signature strongly depends on a multitude of factors such as the psychophysical state of the signer and its social and cultural environment as well as the conditions under which the signature acquisition process occurs.[3,5] The result is that several basic aspects concerned with handwritten signature are still open to investigation. Among others, signature stability is currently at the centre of a large debate. In fact, everyone is aware that his/her signature is never the same even if each of us generally learns to sign at an early age and practices constantly to produce similar signatures according to his/her specific and personal model. Hence, stability in handwritten signatures is a crucial characteristic for investigating the intrinsic human properties related to handwriting generation processes concerning human psychology and biophysics. In addition, research on signature stability can provide new insights for a more accurate design of signature verification systems.[5]

In the scientific literature, approaches for the analysis of local stability in handwritten signature can be classified into three categories.

Approaches of the first category perform stability analyses on raw data. Examples of these approaches can be found with respect to both online and offline signatures. When online signatures are considered, a local stability function can be obtained by using Dynamic Time Warping (DTW) to match a genuine signature against other authentic specimens. Each matching is used to identify the Direct Matching Points (DMPs), that are unambiguously matched points of the genuine signature. Thus, a DMP can indicate the presence of a small stable region in the signature, since no significant distortion has been locally detected. The local stability of a signature point is determined as the average number of time it is a DMP, when the signature is matched against other genuine signatures. Following this procedure low- and high-stability regions can be identified[6,7,8] and usefully considered for selecting reference signatures[9,10] and implementing a verification strategy.[11,12] In another approach based on the handwriting generation and motor control studies, stability regions are defined as the longest common sequences of strokes between a pair of genuine signatures.[13] When offline signatures are considered, the degree of stability of each signature region can be estimated by a multiple pattern-matching technique.[14,15] In this case, corresponding regions of genuine signatures are matched in order to estimate the extent to which they are locally similar. Of course, a preliminary step is used to determine the best alignment of the corresponding regions of signatures, in order to diminish any differences among them. Optical flow has also been used to estimate stability of offline signatures by investigating the shape deformation among genuine specimens[16,17] as well as considering the characteristics of the displacement vector fields.[18,19]

Approaches of the second type use a signature model and perform the analysis of stability considering model parameters. For instance, a client-entropy measure has been proposed to group and characterize signatures in categories that can be related to signature variability and complexity. This measure based on local density estimated using a Hidden Markov Model (HMM) can be used to assess whether a signature contains or not enough information to be successfully processed by any verification system.[20]

Approaches of the third category perform stability analyses on the basis of a set of features extracted from signatures. Indeed, when considering online signatures, many approaches estimate signature stability by the analysis of a specific set of characteristics. In general, these approaches have shown that there is a set of features which remain stable over long time periods, while others can change significantly in time.[21,22] More precisely, a comparative study of the consistency of dynamic signatures has demonstrated that position, velocity and pen inclination can be considered to be among the most consistent features when a distance-based consistency model is applied.[21] Concerning static signatures, another approach uses a multiple-matching strategy in which feature vectors extracted from corresponding regions of genuine specimens are matched through cosine similarity.[23,24]

This paper presents a new technique, which can be classified in the second type of approaches, for the analysis of local stability in online signatures. From the Sigma-Lognormal representation of handwritten signature apposition, the velocity profiles are matched by Dynamic Time Warping (DTW) and local stability analysis is performed by studying the (optimal) warping function. The organization of the paper is the following. The Sigma-Lognormal model is presented in Section 2. Section 3 presents the technique for the analysis of stability based on Dynamic Time Warping. Section 4 presents the experimental results, carried out on signatures of the SuSig database. Section 5 presents the conclusion of the work.

2. The Sigma-Lognormal Model

The kinematic theory of rapid human movement,[25] relies on the Sigma-Lognormal model to represent the information of both the motor commands and timing properties of the neuromuscular system involved in the production of complex movements like signatures.[26] The Sigma-Lognormal model considers the resulting speed of a single stroke j as having a lognormal shape Λ scaled by a command parameter (D) and time-shifted by the time occurrence of the command (t_0):

$$\left|v_j(t;P_j)\right| = D_j \Lambda(t-t_{0j};\mu_j,\sigma_j^2) = \frac{D_j}{\sigma(t-t_{0j})\sqrt{2\pi}} \exp\left\{\frac{\left[\ln(t-t_{0j})-\mu_j\right]^2}{-2\sigma_j^2}\right\} \quad (1)$$

where $P_j=[D_j, t_{0j}, \mu_j, \sigma_j, \theta_{sj}, \theta_{ej}]$ represents the sets of Sigma-Lognormal parameters:[26]

- D_j: amplitude of the input commands;

- t_{0j}: time occurrence of the input commands, a time-shift parameter;

- μ_j: log-time delays, the time delay of the neuromuscular system expressed on a logarithmic time scale;

- σ_j: log-response times, which are the response times of the neuromuscular system expressed on a logarithmic time scale;

- θ_{sj}: starting angle of the circular trajectories described by the jth lognormal stroke;

- θ_{ej}: ending angle of the circular trajectories described by the jth lognormal stroke.

Additionally, from the hypothesis that every lognormal stroke represents the movement as happening along pivot (i.e. producing circle-arc trajectories), the angular position can be computed as[26]:

$$\phi_j(t;P_j) = \theta_{sj} + \frac{\theta_{ej}-\theta_{sj}}{D_j} \int_0^t \left|v(\tau;P_j)\right|d\tau \quad (2)$$

According to this model, a signature can be seen as the output of a generator that produces a set of individual strokes superimposed in time. The resulting complex trajectories can be modeled as a vector summation of lognormal distributions (N_{LN} being the total number of lognormal strokes composing the handwritten trace)[25]:

$$\vec{v}(t) = \sum_{j=1}^{N} \left|\vec{v_j}(t;P_j)\right| \begin{bmatrix} cos(\phi_j(t;P_j)) \\ sin(\phi_j(t;P_j)) \end{bmatrix} \quad (3)$$

3. Analysis of Signature Stability

In this paper a local stability function is defined starting from the analysis of handwritten signatures in the generation domain, as suggested in [27]. More precisely, let $S = \{S^r \mid r=1,2,\ldots,n\}$ be a set of n signatures from the same writer. According to the Sigma-Lognormal model (see eqs. (1–3)), a signature S^t of S is here represented by a sequence

$$S^r = (z^r_1, z^r_2, z^r_3, \ldots z^r_j, \ldots, z^r_m) \tag{4}$$

where $z^r_j = (t_j, v_j(t_j))$ describes synthetically the j-th lognormal stroke in which the signature is decomposed, t_j being the time for which the velocity $v_j(t)$ is maximum and $v_j(t_j)$ the value of the maximum of the velocity profile. Now, let S^r and S^t be two signatures of S. A warping function between S^r and S^t is any sequence of index pairs identifying points of S^r and S^t to be joined:

$$W(S^r, S^t) = C^1, C^2, \ldots C^k \tag{5}$$

where $C^k = (i^k, j^k)$ (k, i^k, j^k integers, $1 \leq k \leq K$, $1 \leq i^k \leq M^r$, $1 \leq j^k \leq M^t$).
   Now, if we consider a distance measure

$$D(C^k) = d(z^r_{ik}, z^t_{jk}) \tag{6}$$

between points of S^r and S^t, we can associate to the warping function in (5) the dissimilarity measure

$$D\big(W(S^r, S^t)\big) = \sum_{k=1}^{K} d(C^k) \tag{7}$$

The elastic matching procedure determine the warping function

$$W^*(S^r, S^t) = C^{*1}, C^{*2}, \ldots, C^{*K} \tag{8}$$

which satisfies the monotonicity, continuity and boundary conditions, and for which the matching distance is minimum [6]:

$$D(W^*(S^r,S^t)) = \min{}_{W(S^r, S^t)} W^*(S^r,S^t) \tag{9}$$

From the warping function W^* of eq. (9), we identify the Direct Matching Strokes (DMS) of S^r with respect to S^t [6, 7]. In particular, in the generation domain, a DMS of a signature S^r with respect to S^t is a lognormal stroke of S^r which has a one-to-one coupling with a lognormal stroke of S^t. In other words, let z^r_p be a stroke of S^r coupled with z^t_q of S^t; z^r_p is DMS of S^r with respect to S^t iff [6, 7]:

- $\quad \forall\ p' = 1,....,M^r$, it results that $z^r_{p'}$ is not coupled with z^t_q;   (10a)

- $\quad \forall\ q' = 1,....,M^t$, it results that $z^t_{q'}$ is not coupled with z^r_p;   (10b)

Now, a DMS indicates the existence of a stroke of the generation process of the r-th signature which is roughly similar to the corresponding stroke of the t-th signature. Therefore, for each stroke of index p of S^r, a score is introduced according to its type of coupling with respect to the corresponding stroke of S^t [8]:

- $\quad Score^t(z^r_p) = 1$ if z^r_p is a DMS   (11a)

- $\quad Score^t(z^r_p) = 0$ if z^r_p is not a DMS   (11b)

Of course, when the genuine signature S^t is matched against all the other genuine signatures of the set S, we can derive the local stability function for each lognormal stroke of S^t, by averaging the scores obtained from eqs. (11) as follows:

$$L\left(z_p^r\right) = \frac{1}{n-1}\sum_{\substack{t=1 \\ t \neq r}}^{n} Score^t(z_p^r) \qquad (12)$$

The global stability function for the signature S^t can be defined as:

$$G(z^r) = \frac{1}{m}\sum_{j=1}^{m} L(z_j^r) \qquad (13)$$

4. Experimental Results

The experimental test was carried out using the Visual SubCorpus of the SuSig database. The Visual SubCorpus is composed by 10 genuine signatures and 10 forgery signatures, acquired by 94 authors.[28] For each signature, Sigma-Lognormal parameters were extracted using the "Robust X_0" algorithm.[26] Figure 1 shows an example of parameter extraction for a signature of the SuSig database. Figure 1 also reports the velocity profile of the signature apposition process, based on the Sigma-Lognormal strokes.

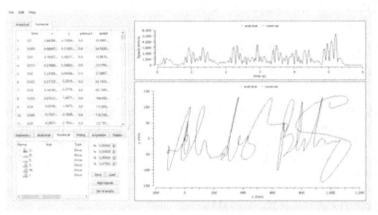

Fig. 1. Parameter Extraction by ScriptStudio.

It is worth noting that the number of lognormal strokes underlying a forgery signature is generally higher than the number of strokes underlying the corresponding genuine specimen, as Table 1 shows with respect to the first 20 authors of the SuSig database.

Table 1. Number of log-normal strokes extracted from signatures.

Author	Genuine		Forgeries	
	Min	*Max*	*Min*	*Max*
1	14	21	16	44
2	20	28	23	54
3	10	15	12	23
4	12	17	18	31
8	24	30	29	41
9	15	29	24	70
10	26	36	28	51
11	25	33	27	39
13	37	54	33	56
14	18	31	30	42
15	21	31	23	35
16	8	15	14	40
17	24	35	34	54
18	42	44	24	37
19	24	34	24	56
20	44	58	51	73

In particular the average number of lognormal strokes is 27.23 for genuine signatures whereas it is 36.13 for forgeries. This can be explained with the presence of additional strokes that are generated by the forger in his attempt to imitate particularly complex traits of the genuine signature.

For the analysis of local stability of the generation process a well-defined Matlab function was implemented with the following purposes:

(i) determine time and velocity profile for the target signature, that is the first signature produced by an author;

(ii) determine time and velocity profile for signatures that must be matched with the target signature;

(iii) determine the warping path using Dynamic Time Warping (TDW);

(iv) compute the local stability function for each stroke (see eq. (12));

(v) compute the global stability for each signature (see eq. (13))

Figure 2 shows the local stability function of a genuine signature, according to the procedure reported in Section 3. For each stroke underlying the signature apposition process, the degree of local stability is shown.

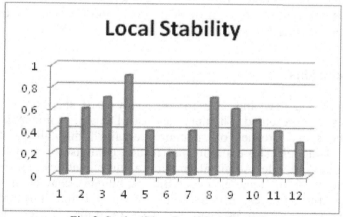

Fig. 2. Stroke (St) vs Local Stability (LS).

The result shows that some strokes exist in which stability of genuine signatures is very high. Conversely, some parts of the signature exist in which the author is not stable in signing. Figure 3 shows the average stability of the signatures of ten different signers. It is easy to verify that some signers are intrinsically more stable than others in signing.

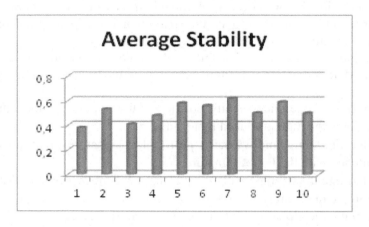

Fig. 3. Signer (Sig) vs Average Stability (AS) in Signing.

Regarding the global stability, figure 3 shows the results obtained by 10 signers, taken randomly from the 94 authors of Visual Subcorpus. For each author, the averaged value of the global stability function of their signatures is reported, which provides information about the stability of the signatures of each signer.

5. Conclusions

In this paper, a new approach for the analysis of stability for online signatures was presented. The approach uses Dynamic Time Warping to match the speed profiles of signatures obtained through the Sigma-Lognormal model. The experimental results demonstrate that the new approach can provide useful information about signatures and it is also capable to point out some characteristics on human behavior in signing. Of course, further research is necessary to verify if this information on stable parts of signatures, can be used to define better signature verification strategies.

References

1. D. Impedovo, G. Pirlo, "Automatic Signature Verification — The State of the Art", IEEE Transactions on Systems, Man and Cybernetics — Part C: Applications and Review, Vol. 38, No. 5, Sept. 2008, pp. 609–635.
2. R. Plamondon and G. Lorette, "Automatic Signature Verification and Writer Identification — The State of the Art", Pattern Recognition, Vol. 22, No. 2, Jan. 1989, pp. 107–131.
3. R. Plamondon, G. Pirlo, D. Impedovo, "Online Signature Verification", D. Doermann and K. Tombre (eds.), Handbook of Document Image Processing, and Recognition, Springer, Berlin, 2013.
4. C. Vielhauer, "A Behavioural Biometrics", Public Service Review: European Union, 2005, no. 9, pp. 113–115.
5. D. Impedovo, G. Pirlo, R. Plamondon, "Handwritten Signature Verification: New Advancements and Open Issues", Proc. XIII International Conference on Frontiers in Handwriting Recognition (ICFHR 2012), Monopoli, Bari, Italy, 18-20 Sept. 2012, pp. 365–370.
6. G. Congedo, G. Dimauro, S. Impedovo, G. Pirlo, "A new methodology for the measurement of local stability in dynamical signatures", Proc. 4th Int. Workshop on Frontiers in Handwriting Recognition (IWFHR-4), 1994, Taipei, Taiwan, pp. 135–144.
7. K. Huang, H. Yan, "Stability and style-variation modeling for on-line signature verification", Pattern Recognition, Vol. 36, No. 10, Oct. 2003, pp. 2253–227.
8. G. Dimauro, S. Impedovo, R. Modugno, G. Pirlo, L. Sarcinella, "Analysis of Stability in Hand-Written Dynamic Signatures", 8th International Workshop on Frontiers in Handwriting Recognition (IWFHR-8), Ontario, Niagara-on-the-Lake, Canada, Aug. 2002, pp. 259–263.
9. V. Di Lecce, G. Dimauro, A. Guerriero, S. Impedovo, G. Pirlo, A. Salzo, L. Sarcinella, "Selection of Reference Signatures for Automatic Signature Verification", 5th Int. Conf. on Document Analysis and Recognition (ICDAR-5), 1999, Bangalore, India, pp. 597–600.
10. G. Pirlo, "Algorithms for Signature Verification", in S. Impedovo (ed.), Fundamentals in Handwriting Recognition, Springer Verlag, Berlin Heidelberg, pp. 435–459.
11. S. Impedovo, G. Pirlo, "Verification of Handwritten Signatures: an Overview", Proc. 14th International Conference on Image Analysis and Processing — ICIAP 2007, IEEE Computer Society Press, September, 11-13, 2007, Modena, Italy, pp. 191–196.
12. D. Impedovo, G. Pirlo, "On-line Signature Verification by Stroke-Dependent Representation Domains", Proc. 12th Int. Conf. Frontiers in Handwriting Recognition (ICFHR-12), Nov. 16-18, 2010, Kolkata, India, pp. 623–627.
13. A. Marcelli, S. G. Fuschetto, A. Parziale, "Modeling Stability in On-line Signatures", Proc. 16th Biennial Conference of the International Graphonomics Society — IGS, At Nara, Japan, 2013.
14. D. Impedovo, G. Pirlo, "On the Measurement of Local Stability of Handwriting — An application to Static Signature Verification", Proc. Biometric Measurements and

Systems for Security and Medical Applications (BIOMS 2010), September, 9, 2010, Taranto, Italy, IEEE Computer Society Press, pp. 41–44.

15. D. Impedovo, G. Pirlo, E. Stasolla, C.A. Trullo, "Learning Local Correspondences for Static Signature Verification", Proc. 11th Int. Conf. of the Italian Association for Artificial Intelligence (AI*IA 2009), December 9-12, 2009, Reggio Emilia, Italy.

16. Y. Mizukami, K. Tadamura, M. Yoshimura, I. Yoshimura, "Statistical Displacement Analysis for Handwriting Verification". Proc. ICIAP 2005, Reggio Emilia, Italy, pp.1174–1181.

17. Y. Mizukami, H. Miike, M. Yoshimura, I. Yoshimura, "An Off-line Signature Verification System using an Extraction Displacement Function", Proc. ICDAR 1999, Bangalore, India, pp.757–760.

18. D. Impedovo, G. Pirlo, "Static Signature Verification by Optical Flow Analysis", Proc. of the 1st International Workshop on Automated Forensic Handwriting Analysis, Beijing, China, September 17-18, 2011, pp. 31–35.

19. G. Pirlo, D. Impedovo, "The Verification of Static Signatures by Optical Flow Analysis", IEEE Trans. on Human-Machine Systems, 2013, vol. 43, p. 499–505.

20. N. Houmani, S. Garcia-Salicetti, B. Dorizzi, "On assessing the robustness of pen coordinates, pen pressure and pen inclination to time variability with personal entropy", Proc. of IEEE 3rd International Conference on Biometrics: Theory, Applications, and Systems, 2009 (BTAS '09), Washington, DC, Sept. 28-30, 2009, pp. 1–6.

21. H. Lei, V. Govindaraju, "A comparative study on the consistency of features in on-line signature verification", Pattern Recognition Letters, Vol. 26, 2005, pp. 2483–2489.

22. L. R. B. Schomaker, R. Plamondon, "The Relation between Axial Pen Force and Pen-Point Kinematics in Handwriting", Biological Cybernetics, vol. 63, pp. 277–289, 1990.

23. D. Impedovo, G. Pirlo, L. Sarcinella, E. Stasolla, C.A.Trullo, "Analysis of Stability in Static Signatures using Cosine Similarity", Proc. XIII International Conference on Frontiers in Handwriting Recognition (ICFHR 2012), Monopoli, Bari, Italy, 18–20 Sept. 2012, pp. 231–235.

24. G. Pirlo, D. Impedovo, "Cosine Similarity for Analysis and Verification of Static Signatures", IET Biometrics, vol. 2, 2014, pp. 151–158.

25. M. Djioua, R. Plamondon, "Studying the Variability of Handwriting Patterns using the Kinematic Theory", Human Movement Science, vol. 28, no. 5, October 2009, pp. 588–601.

26. C. O'Reilly, R. Plamondon, "Development of a Sigma-Lognormal Representation for On-Line Signatures. Pattern Recognition, vol.42, 2009, pp. 3324–3337.

27. G. Pirlo, D. Impedovo, "Stability of dynamic signatures: from the representation to the generation domain", Petrosino A (ed.), Proc. ICIAP 2013, LNCS, Springer, Berlin, 2013.

28. B. Yanikoglu, A. Kholmatov, "SUSIG: an online handwritten signature database, associated protocol and benchmark results", Pattern Anal. Applications, 2009, Vol. 12, pp. 227–236.

CHAPTER 2

EXPLOITING STABILITY REGIONS FOR ONLINE SIGNATURE VERIFICATION

Antonio Parziale, Angelo Marcelli

DIEM, University of Salerno
Via Giovanni Paolo II, 132, 84084 Fisciano (SA), Italy
E-mail: {anparziale, amarcelli}@unisa.it

We present a method for finding the stability regions within a set of genuine signatures and for selecting the most suitable ones to be used for online signature verification. The definition of stability region builds upon motor learning and adaptation in handwriting generation, while their selection exploits both their ability to model signing habits and their effectiveness in capturing distinctive features. The stability regions represent the core of a signature verification system whose performance is evaluated on a standard benchmark.

1. Introduction

Signatures, as any handwriting, are obtained by concatenating elementary movements, or strokes, in such a way that their execution requests the minimum amount of metabolic energy. Such an optimization is learned along the years by repeated practice, so that signing becomes automated and can be performed, at least partially, without any visual feedback, as it was an elementary movement. When the signature has been completely learned, i.e. it becomes a distinctive feature of the subject, it is stored in the brain as a motor plan that incorporates both the sequence of target points, i.e. the points where two successive strokes join, and the sequence of motor commands to be executed to draw the desired shape between them.[1] The encoding of such a motor plan, moreover, is independent of the actuator.[2]

13

According to those findings, multiple executions of the signature by the subject may produce ink traces with different shapes only because of variations on both the psychophysical conditions of the subject and the signing conditions, since the motor plan remains the same.[3,4] It is also expected, however, that the variations in the signing conditions mentioned above may affect only some of the signature features, but not all of them. For this reason, one of the aspects around which is centered the research activity in the field of signature verification is the detection of stability regions, which are the traits of ink that are shared by different executions of the signature.

Signature stability can be estimated directly from the signature signal or indirectly on the set of features used for representing the signature.[3] Among the methods for directly estimating on-line signature stability, those using DTW to derive a local stability function,[5,6] are the most similar to the one presented in this paper, in that the analysis of local stability is used to select the best subset of reference signatures.

In this work we present a method for the detection of stability regions in online signatures. The proposed method assumes as stability regions the longest common sequences of similar strokes between pairs of signatures. This assumption follows from the observation that, as discussed above, signing is the automated execution of a well-learned motor task, and therefore repeated executions should produce, at least ideally, the same movements, which, in turn, should produce ink traces with the same shape. Because of the variations in the signing conditions, it happens that the ink traces are different, but because they results from the execution of the same motor plan, and because the effects of different initial conditions in signing attenuate quickly during writing, it is expected that only short sequences of strokes will exhibit different shapes. The longer the sequence of similar strokes the longer the time during which the same motor program is executed under the same conditions.

Once the stability regions of the genuine signatures have been found, they are used to compute a features representation of the questioned signature. Such a representation is achieved by evaluating the longest common sequence of similar strokes between the ink trace of the questioned and those of the genuine containing the selected stability regions.

The remaining of the paper is organized as it follows. In section 2 we illustrate the method for finding the stability regions between a pair of signatures, and how they can be used for selecting the reference signatures. The selected reference signatures and their associated stability regions are then used in a signature verification experiment reported in section 3. Eventually, in the conclusion we discuss the performance achieved by the proposed method and outline our future research.

2. Modeling Stability in Signatures

According to the definition given above, stability regions should correspond to pieces of ink produced while aiming at reaching the sequence of target points stored in the trajectory plan by using the motor commands stored in the motor plan to draw the desired shapes. Then, the stability region between two signatures is represented by the two sequence of strokes, one on each signatures, with similar shape and aiming at reaching the same target points. In the following we will introduce the algorithm we have designed for finding the stability region between two signatures.

2.1. *Searching for stability regions between two signatures*

The proposed method assumes that the signature signal has been segmented into a sequence of strokes, each of which has been label as ascender, descender or normal, and detects the stability region by an ink matcher that finds the longest common sequences of strokes with similar shapes between the ink traces of a pair of signatures.

For deciding when two sequences are similar enough, i.e. when they match, the method exploits the concept of saliency that has been proposed to account for attentional gaze shift in primate visual system.[8] Accordingly, sequence of strokes that are "globally" more similar than other will stand out in the saliency map.

To implement such an approach one needs to define a scale space, to find a similarity measure to be adopted at each scale, to compute the saliency map, and eventually to select the matching pieces of ink representing the stability region. Figure 1 illustrates the implementation steps. For the sake of clarity, the strokes are line segments instead of curve segments, as in the more general case. We have adopted as scale the number of strokes in the sequences whose similarity is being measured. Such a number will be referred in the following as the *length* of the sequence. In case the two sequences under comparison have N and M strokes, then the number of scales corresponds to the length $K = min(N,M)$ and successive scales are obtained considering sequences made of $k = K,K-1,...,2$ strokes.[9]

As similarity measure, we adopt the Weighted Edit Distance (WED), which assumes that each stroke is represented by a polygonal approximation of the corresponding signature signal and measures the shape dissimilarity WED_{ij} between the i_{th} strokes of one signature and the j_{th} strokes of the other one by evaluating the curvature variations between the polylines associated to the strokes[10]. By definition, WED_{ij} equals 0 for identical strokes, and lower values of WED_{ij} corresponds to more similar strokes. WED_{ij} is therefore an array of N×M values. From WED_{ij} we eventually compute the similarity between two strokes, denoted by W_{ij} as:

$$W_{ij} = (8 - WED_{ij})/8 \tag{1}$$

so that $W_{ij}=1$ for identical stroke, while $W_{ij}=0$ for the most different pairs of strokes, i.e. two strokes with the same shape but opposite direction and concavity (Fig.1.b).

Then, the shape similarity between two sequences at scale k is obtained by adding the shape similarities of the k diagonal elements of W_{ij} starting from i,j and computing their average:

$$W_{ij}^k = \sum_{p=0}^{k-1} W_{i+p,j+p} /k \tag{2}$$

With such a notation, W^k_{ij} represents the shape similarity of the sequences of k strokes starting from the i_{th} stroke of one signature and from the j_{th} stroke of the other one. It is, therefore, an array of $N-k, M-k$ values, as shown in fig. 1.c.

The saliency map is then obtained by a two steps procedure that first selects the most salient sequence(s) at each scale and then combines them into the final one(s). In the first step, at each scale we select the most salient sequences of strokes as those sequences that include the pair(s) of strokes i,j corresponding to $max(W^k_{ij})$. The saliency of the strokes belonging to such sequences is given by:

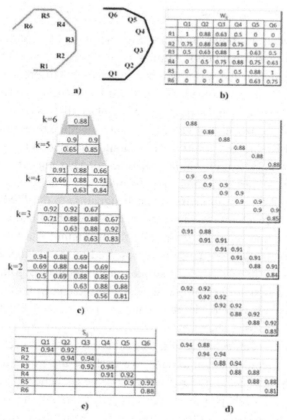

Fig. 1. The procedure for finding the stability regions. a) the shapes under comparison; b) the stroke shape similarity array W_{ij}; c) the pyramid of stroke sequence shape similarity arrays W^k_{ij}; d) the saliency map at each scale; e) the final saliency map.

$$S^k_{ij} = \max\left(W^k_{i-k,j-k}, \dots, W^k_{i,j}\right), \Leftrightarrow W^k_* \neq null \qquad (3)$$

while the saliency of all the other pairs of strokes is set to *null*, as shown in figure 1.d. In the second step we compute the saliency map $S(N,M)$ by assigning to each element corresponding to a pair of strokes that has been included in the most salient sequences detected at different scales the value corresponding to its largest saliency across the scales:

$$S_{ij} = \max\left(S_{ij}^k\right), \forall\, i,j \colon S_{ij}^k \neq null \qquad (4)$$

In such a way, as shown in figure 1.e, each pair of strokes receives a values that takes into account how similar are the strokes and how often they have been included in the most salient sequences at different scales. The saliency map is then thresholded for selecting the longest similar sequence of strokes (LSSS), i.e. the sequences of strokes that correspond to the longest diagonal sequence(s) of values S_{ij} greater than the threshold S_{th}.

As previously said, a stability region should correspond to sequences of strokes that not only exhibit similar shapes, but also aim at reaching the same sequence of target points. To estimate to which extent the two sequences of strokes corresponding on each signature to the *LSSS*, let us say *S1* and *S2* aim at reaching the same sequence of target points, we represent each stroke by a line segment connecting the beginning and the end of the stroke. In this way, each sequence is represented by a polyline, made of as many segments as the number S of strokes in the sequence, going from the beginning of the first strokes of the sequence to the end of the last one, and whose sequence of vertices is the sequence of the segmentation points between the stroke, and therefore provide, according to our conjecture on signature generation, an estimate of the target points of the trajectory plan.

With such a representation at hand, we evaluate the extent to which the two sequence S1 and S2 aim at reaching the same sequence of target points as it follows. For each pair of successive segments of the polyline, we compute the angle α_s between the s_{th} and $(s+1)_{th}$ segments, with $s=1,...,S-1$. Then, we compute the difference $\Delta\alpha_s = \alpha^1_s - \alpha^2_s$, where α^1_s and α^2_s are the sequence of angles computed as above on the two polylines associated to *S1* and *S2*, respectively. We eventually compute the similarity of the sequence of target points of *S1* and *S2* as:

$$T_s = \gamma * \cos\left(2\Delta\alpha_h\right) \qquad (5)$$

where γ is a constant. At this point we can combine the two measures we have, the shape similarity W_s and the target point similarity T_s, to select the sequences of strokes corresponding to the deride stability region. Given a *LSSS* that goes from stroke S_b to stroke S_e, we can compute its *global similarity GS* as:

$$GS = \sum_{h=S_b}^{S_e} W_h * T_h \qquad (6)$$

where W_h denotes the shape similarity of the sequence. Eventually, the desired stability regions are the *LSSS* whose global similarity is greater than a threshold GS_{th}, as shown in (Fig. 2).

2.2. *Searching for stability regions in a set of signatures*

The procedure described in the previous Section computes the stability region between a pair of signatures. In way of principle, one would expect that the same stability region appear in all the signatures of a subject, and therefore would define the stability region of a set of signatures as the longest common subsequences of the stability regions computed for every available pair of signatures. In practice, however, both the stroke segmentation and the ink matching may introduce errors in locating the segmentation points and/or in deciding when a sequence of strokes is similar to another, that may produce different stability regions for the set of signatures. When this happens, it is necessary to define a criterion either for selecting among the stability regions the best one, i.e the pair of signatures that capture at the best the signing habits of the subject, or for combining them.

Fig. 2. The segmentation points (dots) and the stability regions (bold) of two signatures.

3. Using the Stability Regions for Signature Verification

According to our definition of stability regions, they are meant to capture the signing habits of a subject, and therefore the verification of a signature should be achieved by evaluating how much of the stability region is found in the specimen under verification: the larger the overlap the higher the chance that the questioned was produced by the same author of the genuine ones. In this way, the stability regions represents the only information used and therefore the success rate will provide a direct evaluation of their effectiveness in capturing the signing habits of the subject.

To implement this idea, we consider that the reference signatures corresponding to the stability region can be interpreted as the dimension of the subject *signature space* Σ. In such a space, each signature can be mapped to the point of coordinate:

$$r_i = \frac{L_m(f, ref_i)}{L_s(ref_i)} \quad i = 1, ..., N \tag{7}$$

In equation (7), L_m is the length of the longest common sequence of strokes between the signature under verification f and the reference ref_i and L_s is the length of the stability region found in ref_i. Each r_i ranges between 0 and 1. To visually illustrate the property of such a space, let's consider the case $N=2$. In such a case, Σ assumes the shape of a square, whose vertices are (0,0), (0,1), (1,0) and (1,1). In such a space, genuine signatures should have a (long) match with the stability regions of both references, and therefore should be represented by points close to the vertex of coordinates (1,1). On the contrary, non-genuine signatures should not have a (long) match with any of the stability regions of the references, and therefore should be represented by points near to the vertex of coordinates (0,0). Thus, the larger the overlap between the questioned signature and the stability regions, the higher the chance the questioned has been produced by the same author of the references. Such a space also allows for a simple implementation of a rule for deciding whether a questioned signature is genuine or not, depending of its actual position in the *signature space*. To this purpose, we compute on a training set including both genuine and non-genuine signatures, the thresholds T_g and T_f, which are the boundary of genuine and non-genuine decision regions, as shown in figure 3. By denoting with d_f and d_g the distances between the point representing a signature and the two vertices (0,0) and (1,1), respectively, the decision criterion follows naturally from above: a signature is considered genuine if it is within the genuine region, or it lies between the two regions and is closer to the genuine region than to the non-genuine one. Thus, the references signatures, their stability regions and the values of T_g and T_f are our model of the author of the genuine signatures with respect to the authors of the non-genuine signatures. In the general case of $N>2$, Σ is an hypercube, and the definition of both the thresholds and the decision rule are obtained by generalization.

4. Experimental Results

In the current implementation of the method, there are three parameters that needs to be set: the constant γ in equation (5), the threshold S_{th} and the threshold GS_{th}. Therefore, we have performed a set of experiments for evaluating the effects of the values of the thresholds, while setting $\gamma =1$ for all of them.

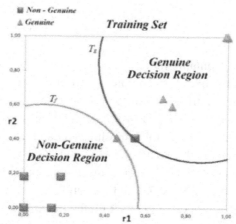

Fig. 3. The training set and the decision regions for genuine and non-genuine

4.1. *The datasets*

The performance of the proposed method has been evaluated on the signatures of SVC2004 database[11] and on the signatures of the Blind subcorpus of the SUSIG database.[12] The first contains 20 genuine and 20 forgery signatures for each of 100 subjects, for a total of 40,000 specimen divided in training set, which is publicly available, and test sets that is not available. The second database contains 10 genuine and 10 forgery signatures for each of 60 subjects.

The experiments on the SVC2004 have been performed by following the protocol proposed during the *First International Signature Verification Competition*[11] for both the training stage and the testing one:

- Skilled forgery detection: for each subject the genuine signatures are randomly divided in two disjoined subsets: 5 samples are used together with 5 forgery signatures as training set, the remaining are added to the set of forgery signatures and used as test set;

- Random forgery detection: the training set is built as before, whereas the test set includes as forgery 20 genuine signatures produced by 20 different subjects

4.2. *Results*

Since the datasets contain more than two genuine signatures, the experiments have been executed combining different criteria to select the best stability regions and different values of S_{th} and GS_{th}.

In this study, we have restricted the experiments to the cases when $N=2$ and $N=3$. Moreover, the values of the thresholds S_{th} and GS_{th} were chosen by using a grid search with $S_{th}=(0.70\div1.0)$ and $GS_{th}=(0.40\div0.80)$. The experiments on the SVC2004 dataset showed that the best results were obtained using $S_{th}=0.9$, $GS_{th}=0.75$ and selecting as references the two genuine signatures that minimize the EER on the training set. The test on the SUSig dataset confirmed that the best performance was obtained by selecting the references as above, whereas the best values for the parameters were $S_{th}=0.9$ and $GS_{th}=0.5$. The difference between the two settings can be explained by noting that the signatures are shorter and therefore segmented in a smaller number of strokes than the samples of the SVC2004 database and then shorter stability regions are obtained. By relaxing the constraint on the global similarity, longer regions are obtained that, as expected, better capture the signing habits of the subjects. Although the main purpose of this paper was not that eventually design a top performing verification system, the comparison of the performance of our method in its best configuration in comparison with those participating in the SVC2004 benchmark, reported in Table 1 show that the proposed method compares favorably with many of the competitors.

5. Conclusions

We have presented a model for describing the signing habit of a subject centered upon the concept of the stability regions, that have been derived by looking at the signature as the output of a learned motor task, according to which the signature is stored in a twofold form, as a sequence of target points and a sequence of motor commands to connect the target points by drawing a line with a given shape.

Based on this conjecture, we have presented a method for finding the stability regions between pairs of signatures and shown how the stability regions can be used to define the *signature space* of a subject. Then, we have proposed a mapping scheme for representing the signatures of the training set in such a space and derived two thresholds for discriminating genuine and non-genuine signatures of a given subject. Accordingly, the signing habits of a subject are represented by its references signatures, their stability regions and the two thresholds. Such a model allow for a simple decision rule that basically evaluated of much of the stability regions of the reference is included in the questioned signatures.

We have evaluated the effectiveness of the proposed definition of stability by performing a signature verification experiment based on a standard protocol and using two standard datasets of online signatures.

The results in Table 1 show that our method ranks 5th in terms of EER_{avg}, but it is the top performing one in terms of SD_{avg}. This latter result confirms that the stability regions capture the signing habits of the subjects because they are the only source of information that has been exploited for both describing the signing habits and for designing a decision rule that is a straightforward implementation of the concept the stability regions are meant to capture.

All together, the experimental results suggest that stability regions as we have defined and implemented do exist in the signatures of a given subject, and that they are capable of capturing the distinctive aspects of signing habit among a population of subject. Thus, the implementations of the stability region provided in Section 2 as well as the decision rule described in Section 3 are a viable tool for implementing top performing system for automatic signature verification. Our future research will focus on optimizing the system configuration by means of an optimization tool, including γ among the set of parameters to be optimized, considering all the stability regions, and removing the heuristic limitations we have adopted in this study on the range of variation for the thresholds S_{th} and GS_{th}. Eventually, we will investigate the behavior of stability regions in case of disguised signatures, that represent the current frontier of the research in the field.

Table 1. Results on SVC2004 database.

Team ID	Skilled forgeries		Random forgeries	
	EER_{avg}	SD_{avg}	EER_{avg}	SD_{avg}
106	5.50%	7.73%	3.65%	4.80%
126	6.45%	10.41%	3.49%	4.53%
124	7.33%	7.71%	2.93%	3.72%
115	9.80%	13.90%	2.90%	3.60%
Our method	**10.94%**	**2.97%**	**4.68%**	**2.38%**
114	11.10%	11.11%	3.36%	4.36%
....	....	....	....	....
112	31.32%	18.09%	11.67%	9.58%

References

1. Senatore, R.: The role of Basal ganglia and Cerebellum in Motor Learning: A computational model. PhD Thesis, University of Salerno (2012, March)
2. Raibert, M. H.: Motor control and learning by state space model. AILab, MIT 1977
3. Impedovo, D., Pirlo, G.: Automatic signature verification: the state of the art. Systems, Man, and Cybernetics, Part C: Applications and Reviews, IEEE Transactions on, 38(5), pp. 609-635 (2008)
4. Impedovo, D., Pirlo, G., Plamondon, R.: Handwritten Signature Verification: New Advancements and Open Issues. In Frontiers in Handwriting Recognition (ICFHR), 2012 International Conference on, pp. 367-372. IEEE, (2012, September)
5. Dimauro, G., Impedovo, S., Modugno, R., Pirlo, G., Sarcinella, L.: Analysis of stability in hand-written dynamic signatures. In Frontiers in Handwriting Recognition, 2002. Proceedings. Eighth International Workshop on, pp. 259-263. IEEE, (2002)
6. Huang, K., Yan, H.: Stability and style-variation modeling for on-line signature verification. Pattern recognition, 36(10), pp. 2253-2270 (2003)
7. Marcelli, A., Fuschetto, S.G., Parziale, A.: Modeling Stability in On-line Signatures. In Proceedings of IGS 2013, pp. 135-138 (2013, June)
8. Itti, L., Koch, C., Niebur, E.: A model of saliency-based visual attention for rapid scene analysis. Pattern Analysis and Machine Intelligence, IEEE Transactions on, 20(11), pp. 1254-1259 (1998)
9. De Stefano, C., Marcelli, A., Santoro, A.: On-line cursive recognition by ink matching. Proceedings of IGS 2007, pp. 23-37 (2007)

10. De Stefano, C., Garruto, M., Lapresa, L., Marcelli, A.: Using strings for on-line handwriting shape matching: a new weighted edit distance. In Image Analysis and Processing, ICIAP 2005, pp. 1125-1132. Springer Berlin Heidelberg (2005)
11. Yeung, D. Y., Chang, H., Xiong, Y., George, S., Kashi, R., Matsumoto, T., Rigoll, G.: SVC2004: First international signature verification competition. In Biometric Authentication, pp. 16-22, Springer Berlin Heidelberg (2004)
12. Kholmatov, A., Yanikoglu, B.: SUSIG: an on-line signature database, associated protocols and benchmark results. Pattern Analysis and Applications, 12(3), pp. 227-236 (2009)

CHAPTER 3

TWO BIOINSPIRED METHODS FOR DYNAMIC SIGNATURES ANALYSIS

Jânio Canuto[1], Bernadette Dorizzi[1], Jugurta Montalvão[2]

*[1]Institut Mines-Telecom, Telecom SudParis, CNRS UMR5157 SAMOVAR
Évry, France
E-mail: {janio.canuto,bernadette.dorizzi}@telecom-sudparis.eu*

*[2]Federal University of Sergipe (UFS), Electrical Engineering Department
São Cristóvão, Sergipe, Brazil
E-mail: jmontalvao@ufs.br*

This work focuses on the problem of dynamic signature segmentation and representation. A brief review of segmentation techniques for online signatures and movement modelling is provided. Two dynamic signature segmentation/representation methods are proposed. These methods are based on psychophysical evidences that led to the well-known Minimum Jerk principle. These methods are alternatives to the existing techniques and are very simple to implement. Experimental evidence indicates that the Minimum Jerk is in fact a good choice for signature representation amongst the family of quadratic derivative cost functions.

1. Introduction

Handwritten signatures result from voluntary but typically complex gestures of the human hand. As result of their particularities, in most cultures, these graphically recorded gestures have been used for centuries to authenticate documents. Some less straightforward uses of handwritten signatures analysis may include mental illness detection or daily stress measurement.[1]

Beyond potential applications, modelling gestures behind signatures and development of proper ways for identification of basic components (i.e., segments) is a challenging enough matter for scientific research. However, segmentation is a crucial step that strongly influences the performance of signature verification systems and, therefore, a special attention has been drawn into this task over the last few decades.[2]

This work aims at providing two new signature segmentation methods, based on psychophysiological evidences that led to the development of the well-known Minimum Jerk principle for movement planning. We focus on dynamic signatures, which are represented as a time series of pen-tip position coordinates acquired through the use of specific recording devices, such as tablets, digitizers or smartphones.

The work is structured as follows: in Section 2 we perform a review of previous works on signature segmentation and movement modelling, with an emphasis on the Minimum Jerk principle. In Section 3 we present the proposed algorithms along with some experimental results. Finally, in Section 4, conclusions are drawn.

2. Previous Works

2.1. *Signature segmentation*

Global features (e.g. length, maxima, minima, and mean velocity) are commonly used in signature verification systems but are not very discriminative. Such features can be made local if applied to *elements* of a segmented signature. Using localized features is sometimes referred to as a stroke-based approach. Although this decomposition has shown to provide good results, it leads to the non-trivial segmentation task.[3]

Indeed, signature segmentation is a very complex task due to the high variability between different signatures provided by the same writer. These variations include stretching, compression, omission and addition of parts of the drawing. Segmentation techniques might derive from specific characteristics of handwriting movements or be more specific for a given matching algorithm. In Impedovo and Pirlo[2] we can find a brief review of such methods that are divided in four categories according to which principle they are based on: pen-up/pen-down signals, velocity analysis, perceptual relevant points and dynamic time warping.

For dynamic signatures, a common and very simple segmentation technique uses pressure information for determining writing units, which are determined as the written part between a pen-down and a pen-up movement.

Segmentation techniques based on velocity analysis use different approaches, ranging from simple detection of null[4] velocity to curvilinear velocity signals. The stroke identification step on the Sigma-Lognormal model[5] can also be placed on such category.

A different class of segmentation methods are those based on the detection of perceptually important points. The importance of a point is determined by the rate of change of the writing angle around it. We can also include in this category techniques based on the detection of geometric extremes.[6]

In order to allow the segmentation of many signatures into the same number of segments, dynamic time warping (DTW) has been widely used.[2]

Combinations of different techniques can also be found in the literature, for instance in Qu *et al.*[7] a combination of pressure (first category), velocity (second category) and angle change (third category) is used for segmentation. Further references for dynamic signature segmentations methods can be found in Impedovo and Pirlo's review paper.[2]

2.2. *Movement modelling*

The study of how the central nervous system (CNS) generates and controls the movement has yielded many computational models, some relying on biological neural network behaviours, artificial neural networks, equilibrium point hypothesis, coupled oscillators and minimization principles.[5]

From a movement planning perspective, the general problem might be posed as follows: It is assumed that human movements are optimally planned according to a latent optimality criterion. Therefore, we need to find what is the optimality criterion used by the CNS. From this formulation, the optimal control theory seems to be the most complete and adequate way for finding an answer.[8]

All minimization principles for movement modelling are part of the optimal control approach. Many optimization criteria have been proposed in the literature and can roughly be divided in four categories: kinematic criteria (e.g. minimum jerk), dynamic criteria (e.g. minimum torque-change), muscular and neural criteria (e.g. minimum effort) and energetic criteria (e.g. minimum total work). A detailed review of such criteria can be found in Berret[8] and references therein. Amongst these criteria, Minimum Jerk (MJ) and Minimum Torque-Change (MTC) are the most used in the literature.

Some of these models have already been used for handwriting representation, but only the sigma-lognormal model, which is based on the kinematics theory of rapid human movement, has been used for signature modelling.[5] On the other hand, we use in our proposed methods the Minimum Jerk principle[9] which to the authors' knowledge has not yet been applied to signature analysis.

Therefore, we now present a more detailed description of the Minimum Jerk principle.

The Minimum Jerk Principle. This model belongs to the category of the quadratic derivative kinematic criteria, which have a general cost function defined as:

$$C = \frac{1}{2} \int_0^T \left(\frac{d^n x(t)}{dt^n}\right)^2 + \left(\frac{d^n y(t)}{dt^n}\right)^2 dt \qquad (1)$$

where T is the movement duration, $x(t)$ and $y(t)$ are the horizontal and vertical position time series respectively. This class of optimum criteria has as general solution polynomials of order $2n - 1$. The *jerk* is defined as the third derivative of the movement, therefore $n = 3$ and the general solution is a fifth-order polynomial. Other well-known kinematic criteria such as acceleration, snap and crackle can be obtained by setting n equal to 2, 4 and 5 respectively.

In Richardson and Flash[9] this family of optimum criteria has been studied up to $n = 10$, and the authors concluded that the Minimum Jerk is the most suitable for human movement modelling. They were able to properly reproduce the two-thirds power law using the minimum jerk. Using the peak to average velocity ratio as a single scalar projection of velocity profiles, they also found that the MJ is the best suited criterion. Indeed, previous experimental evidences showed that this ratio is about 1.8 (with 10% standard deviation) for reaching movements and the MJ yields a ratio of 1.875 for reaching movements.[9]

Some works point that the Minimum Jerk principle is unable to produce asymmetric velocity profiles,[8,10] however this is only true if velocity and acceleration at both the beginning and the end of the movement are null, which is not a requirement of the model itself. Furthermore, in Berret[8] it is noted that MJ predictions are not in agreement with experimental data when the movement occurs on the vertical plane or when the target is not a single point but an infinite set of point (a straight line, for instance); however MJ predictions work properly on the horizontal plane for point-to-point movements. These conditions can both be assumed for a signing movement.

3. Proposed Method

All experiments described in this section have been performed over the MCYT-100 Database,[11] which consists of 25 genuine and 25 forged signatures from 100 different writers. These signatures have been acquired with a Wacom® Tablet at a fixed sample rate of 100Hz. In our experiments, since we are focused on segmentation and representation, and not on verification, only the genuine subset has been used.

Our first segmentation method is based on the peak to mean velocity ratio observed on the psychophysical experiments realized during the developments of the MJ principle.

The signature can be seen as a series of point-to-point reaching movements. We sequentially search for signature segments that comply with the expected 1.8 ratio. This way, this method can be categorized amongst the velocity analysis segment techniques. For a given signature, the algorithm can be described as follows:

   (i)   Compute the instantaneous velocity magnitude, V

  (ii)   Set START = 1, END = START+1, S(1) = 1 and C = 2

 (iii)   Get the velocity, VS, between START and END

 (iv)   Compute the ratio, R, between maximum VS and mean VS

  (v)   If R >= 1.8

        (a) Set S(C) = END

        (b) Set START = END+1, END = START+1 and C = C+1

 (vi)   If R < 1.8 set END = END+1

(vii)   If END <= length of V go to step 3.

(viii)   Return S

This extremely simple procedure provides a stable segmentation amongst different signatures of the same writer, with an average coefficient of variation of the number of segments of 13% for all writers. In Figure 1 are shown some examples of segmentation for five different signatures of two writers on the MCYT-100 Database.

It is interesting noting that using this method we are able to remove small artefacts that are often present at the beginning and end of the acquired signatures. The obtained segmentations roughly correspond to changes in the dynamic behaviour (e.g. loops, waves and straight lines).

Fig. 1. Segmentation of five different signatures of two writers using the velocity ratio criterion.

Visual inspection of the obtained segmentation seems to yield "natural" segments. This technique has the advantages of not being tied to any verification technique, and can be used for any signature analysis task. Furthermore, the 1.8 threshold used for segmentation is based on psychophysical experiments that have been reproduced many times over the last 30 years.

This segmentation does not provide a model for the resulting elements, contrary to what occur with the Sigma-Lognormal model. One could use the result of the MJ principle (i.e. a fifth order polynomial) in order to model each of the resulting segments, however not all of the elements can be properly modelled by such simple functions, resulting in a very poor reconstruction quality, especially on signatures containing many consecutive loops.

The reconstruction quality, measured through the Velocity SNR, as in Plamondon *et al.*,[5] is defined as:

$$SNR_v = 10 \log \left(\frac{\int_0^T [v_x^2(t) + v_y^2(t)] dt}{\int_0^T \left[(v_x(t) - v_{xx}(t))^2 + (v_y(t) - v_{yy}(t))^2 \right] dt} \right) \qquad (2)$$

where $v_x(t)$ and $v_y(t)$ are respectively the horizontal and vertical velocities on the original signature, and $v_{xx}(t)$ and $v_{yy}(t)$ are the horizontal and vertical velocities of the reconstructed signature, respectively. For the abovementioned reconstruction of segments (with fifth order polynomials) an average SNR_V of 10.7 dB is obtained for the MCYT-100 database.

We now propose a second method, based on the MJ Model itself, that result in a piecewise polynomial representation of the signature. This approach models each "writing element" as a fifth order polynomial. The procedure consists in sequentially finding the longer segments that can be adequately represented (according to a given reconstruction quality threshold) by a fifth order polynomial.[12]

Notice that the 1.8 peak to mean velocity ratio is *only* observed on reaching movements, in which starting and ending velocity and acceleration are considered to be null (thus, resulting in a symmetric velocity profile), different boundary conditions on the MJ Model lead to different velocity ratios and velocity profiles. Therefore, fitting the fifth-order polynomial to the signature data allows for a better representation of the velocity profiles and can provide not only segmentation but an adequate representation for each segment. The algorithm for this method can be described as follows:

(i)   Normalize the trajectory through a min-max procedure
(ii) Set $L = 1$
(iii) Set $R = L + 5$
(iv) Fit a 5th order polynomial to the points in the interval $[X(L):X(R)]$
(v)   Calculate the Velocity SNR for the interval
(vi) If SNR $> =$ Threshold
    (c) Set $R = R+1$ and go to step 4.
(vii) If SNR $<$ Threshold
    (d) Set $L = R-1$ and go to step 3.
(viii) If $R >$ length of X, stop.
(ix) Return the list of L values.

This procedure is still very simple but much more computationally intensive than the previous one because of the fitting procedure. We chose not to use the Jerk value itself because the numerical estimation of third order derivatives from time-sampled data leads to large numerical errors. We now have a piecewise polynomial representation of signing movements that can be properly predicted by the MJ model.

One of the advantages of such procedure is that the representation quality can be chosen by the user to fit his/her needs. In Figure 2 we present the segmentation obtained for the signatures shown in Figure 1 with a SNR_v of 15dB.

Even though for the signatures on the right column in Figure 2 we observe more segments than using the first method, on average, for the whole database this procedure produce fewer segments than the previous one. Furthermore, the number of segments obtained for each writer is more stable than before, with a coefficient of variation of the number of segments of 7.3%, that is even lower than the variability for the lengths of the signatures which is of 8%.

Now the obtained signature elements are basically arcs and single loops, most of them containing at least one inflection point. Along with

Fig. 2. Segmentation of five different signatures of two writers using the MJ criterion at 15 dB SNR.

the automatic segmentation we have an alternative representation for the signature as a sequence of fifth order polynomials. Considering the trade-off between compression rate and reconstruction quality, we did experiments similar to those in Richardson and Flash[9] with different cost functions belonging to the family defined by Equation (1), with n ranging from one to five. In this work we define the Compression Rate as the ratio between the difference in bytes of the original and modelled signatures and its original size.

Once again the Minimum Jerk ($n = 3$) seems to be the best option, acting as a limit to the compression — quality trade-off. For a SNR of 15 dB all of the higher order ($n \geq 3$) solutions attain the same compression rate of 73.3%. In Figure 3 we show the compression — quality trade-off curves for each different cost function.

Finally, since we have a compressed representation of the signatures, we believe it is possible to reduce computational costs without losing on overall system performance. On verification experiments performed using DTW for matching we were indeed able to keep the same performance level, with a 0.02% loss in terms of EER (the operational point at which false acceptance error and false rejection rates are the same for a given verification system). DTW was chosen for these

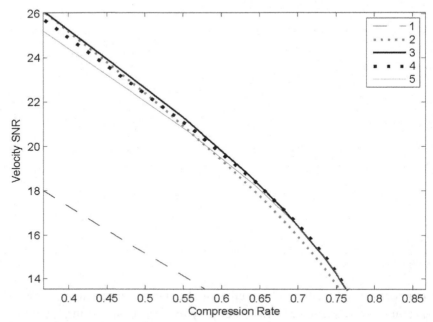

Fig. 3. Representation quality and compression rate tradeoff for minimum velocity ($n = 1$), acceleration ($n = 2$), jerk ($n = 3$), snap ($n = 4$) and crackle ($n = 5$).

experiments because it has yielded the best results on verification systems based only on pen-position information.[2]

However, no significant decrease on computational cost was observed, since the direct use of DTW for matching of the modelled signatures gave poor results a reconstruction step was needed. This experiment suggests that our representation at 15 dB SNR_v has an acceptable quality, keeping most of the discriminative information, but a different technique is needed in order to efficiently exploit such condensed information.

4. Conclusions and Future Work

Two methods for automatic signature segmentation and one for signature representation have been presented. These methods are based on the Minimum Jerk Principle and to the authors knowledge it is the first use of such principle for online signatures. Both methods are very easy to implement and can be used as alternatives to existing methods.

As pointed out before, it is hard to determine if our approaches are better than existing methods because such evaluation strongly depends on what the segmentation/representation is going to be used to. An advantage of the proposed model (2nd method) is the possibility of choosing the desired representation error.

The proposed method can be understood as an alternative use of the Minimum Jerk criterion as a basis function for a piecewise representation. In such way the commonly used velocity and acceleration constraints are not needed as well as any manually inserted via-points.

We believe that the ratio between the number of segments obtained by such method and the original length of the signature may be used as a *"complexity"* measure in a similar fashion to the Normalized Lempel-Ziv Complexity,[13] we have an ongoing work on the demonstration of this link between detected segments and Lempel-Ziv Complexity. Using such measure we were capable of obtaining a similar classification over the MCYT-100 database to that obtained by Garcia-Salicetti *et al.*[14] using the Personal Entropy. We intend to perform further experiments on other databases to verify if there is indeed a correlation between the Personal Entropy and the MJ based complexity measure.

The next step in our work consists in performing further implementations, using different databases and possibly non-latin signatures (*e.g.* Chinese), in order to obtain a higher level assessment of the impact of our method and a better understanding of its advantages and disadvantages.

Furthermore, since the Minimum Jerk principle is derived from the analysis of healthy individuals' movements, this *complexity* measure may be used in the early diagnosis of motor diseases such as Parkinson's and Dyskinesia.

Acknowledgments

This work was partially funded by CAPES. The authors would like to thank Dr. Nesma Houmani for providing the detailed results of her work over the MCYT-100 Database.

References

1. M. P. Caliguri, H.-L. Teulings, J. V. Filoteo, D. Song, J. B. Lohr. Quantitative measurement of handwriting in the assessment of drug-induced parkinsonism. *Human Mov. Sci.*, **25**(4–5), pp. 510–522 (2006).
2. D. Impedovo and G. Pirlo. Automatic signature verification: the state of the art. *IEEE Trans. Syst., Man, and Cybern. — Part C*, **38**(5), pp. 609–635, (2008).
3. K. W. Yue and W. S. Wijesoma. Improved Segmentation and Segment Association for Online Signature Verification. In *Proc. IEEE Int. Conf. Syst., Man, Cybern.*, **4**, pp. 2752–2756 (2000).
4. J. G. A. Dolfing, E. H. L. Aarts and J. J. G. M. von Oosterhout. On-line Signature Verification with Hidden Markov Models. In *Proc. 4th Int. Conf. Pat. Rec.*, **2**, pp. 1309–1312 (1998).
5. R. Plamondon, C. O'Reilly, J. Galbally, A. Almaksour and E. Anquetil. Recent developments in the study of rapid human movements with the kinematic theory: applications to handwriting and signature synthesis. *Pat. Rec. Letters*, In Press: available online 15 June (2012).
6. J. Lee, H.-S. Yoon, J. Soh, B. T. Chun and Y. K. Chung. Using geometric extrema for segment-to-segment characteristics comparison in online signature verification. *Pat. Rec.*, **37**, pp. 93–103 (2004).
7. T. Qu, A. E. Saddik and A. Adler. A stroke based algorithm for dynamic signature verification. In *Proc. Can. Conf. Ele. Comp. Eng. (CCECE)*, pp. 461–464 (2004).
8. B. Berret. *Integration de la force gravitaire dans la planification motrice et le contrôle des mouvements du bras et du corps.* PhD thesis, Bourgogne University, Dijon, France (2008).
9. M. J. E. Richardson and T. Flash. Comparing smooth arm movements with the two-thirds power law and the related segmented-control hypothesis. *J. Neuroscience*, **22**(18), pp. 8201–8211 (2002).
10. M. Dijoua and R. Plamondon. The limit profile of a rapid movement velocity. *Human Movement Science*, **29**(1), pp. 48–61, (2010).
11. J. Ortega-Garcia, J. Fierrez-Aguilar, D. Simon, J. Gonzalez, M. Faundez-Zanuy, V. Espinosa, A. Satue, I. Hermanez, J. J. Igarza, C. Vivaracho, D. Escudero and Q. I. Moro. MCYT baseline corpus: a bimodal biometric database. *IEEE. Proc. Vis., Im., Sig. Proc.*, **150**(6), pp. 395–401 (2003).
12. J. Canuto, B. Dorizzi and J. Montalvão. Dynamic Signatures Representation Using the Minimum Jerk Principle. In *Proc 4th IEEE Biosig. Biorob. Conf.* (ISSNIP), pp. 1–6 (2013).
13. J. Ziv. Coding theorems for individual sequences. *IEEE. Trans. Inf. Theory*, **IT-24**(4), pp. 405–412 (1978).
14. S. Garcia-Salicetti, N. Houmani and B. Dorizzi. A novel criterion for writer enrolment based on a time-normalized signature sample entropy measure. *EURASIP J. on Adv. in Sig. Proc.*, **2009** (2009).

CHAPTER 4

USING GLOBAL FEATURES FOR PRE-CLASSIFICATION IN ONLINE SIGNATURE VERIFICATION SYSTEMS[*]

Marianela Parodi and Juan C. Gómez

Lab. for System Dynamics & Signal Processing, UNR & CIFASIS, Argentina
E-mail: {parodi,gomez}@cifasis-conicet.gov.ar

In this paper, a pre-classification stage based on global features is incorporated to an online signature verification system for the purposes of improving its performance. The pre-classifier makes use of the discriminative power of some global features to discard (by declaring them as forgeries) those signatures for which the associated global features are far away from their respective means. Global features are considered individually and in a combined form for pre-classification. The subsequent classification stage is based on features obtained from a wavelet approximation of the time functions associated with the signing process. The experimental results show that the proposed pre-classification approach is capable of getting error rate improvements with respect to the case where no pre-classification is performed, having also the advantages of simplifying and speeding up the verification process.

1. Introduction

Signature verification is one of the most popular non invasive methods for identity verification.[2] Two categories of signature verification systems can be distinguished taking into account the acquisition device, namely, offline (only the signature image is available) and online systems (dynamic information about the signing process is available).

In online systems, the signature is parameterized by several discrete time functions, such as pen coordinates, pressure and, when available,

---

[*] This paper is an extended version of the EAHSP 2013 Workshop paper.[1]

altitude and azimuth angles. Researchers have long argued about the effectiveness of these time functions for verification purposes.[3] In addition, to select which features could be extracted from the time functions is an important design step. Features can be classified into local, computed for each point in the time sequence, and global, computed from the whole signature. Many researchers accept that approaches based on local features achieve better performance than those based on global ones, but still there are others who favor the use of global features.[4,5] Global features have the advantage of being simple, usually more intuitive than local ones, and easier to compute and compare. Further- more, it would be reasonable to expect that local and global features could provide complementary information,[5] and the way they should be combined is an interesting and still open challenge. A multilevel online signature verification system which uses three different signature repre- sentations, one based on global features and the other two based on local ones, has been presented.[6] Also several decision fusion strategies using local and global features, have been compared.[5] Some approaches using a pre-classification stage based on global features, such as signature total time duration and pen down duration, for the purposes of early detecting bad forgeries, have been proposed in the mid 1990's.[6,7]

In this paper, global based features are used for pre-classification pur- poses. The idea is to pre-classify signatures, declaring as forgeries those that are far away from their mean, in terms of the global based features. This could help to quickly recognize and classify gross forgeries, speeding up and simplifying the verification process. The remaining sig- natures continue with the subsequent classification stage which consists in extracting new features (wavelet approximations of the associated time functions) providing a more detailed representation, and classifying them on the basis of a Random Forest (RF) classifier.[8]

For the verification experiments, two different signature styles are considered, namely, Western and Chinese, of a recent publicly available Signature Databases. Two different approaches for pre-classification are proposed in this paper. On one hand, each global based feature is used separately and its discriminative capacity is analysed. On the other hand, the global based features are used in a combined form (unique feature vector) and their combined discriminative power is studied.

2. Pre-Classification Approach

In this paper, the idea is to exploit the intrinsic characteristics of features based on global parameters and based on time functions for different tasks. When using global based features, it would be expectable to get a rough and quick signature representation that could be useful to detect some anomalies of the signature. On the other hand, if a more precise representation is needed, using the time function based features could provide it, at the cost of a more time consuming feature extraction.

Global based features are then used in this paper for pre-classification purposes. It is reasonable to expect that some global based features, such as signature total time duration, pen down duration and average pressure, for the genuine samples would be far away from the corresponding ones for the forged samples. This is illustrated in Fig. 1 (left), for the case of a single global based feature, where the distributions of the global based feature "signature total time duration" for the genuine (left) and forged (right) signatures of an author in the database, are depicted.

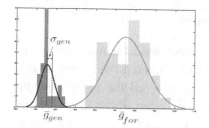

Algorithm 1

If $|g_{test} - \bar{g}_{train}|^2 > \alpha^2 \sigma^2_{train}$

then signature=FORGERY

else continue classification

Fig. 1. Left: Distribution of the global feature "signature total time duration" for the genuine and forged signatures of an author in the database. Right: Decision rule.

The idea is then to classify as a forgery those signatures for which the global based features differ significantly from the corresponding genuine feature mean. In particular, the decision rule in Fig. 1 (right) is considered. There, g_{test} denotes the global based feature corresponding to the test signature, $\bar{g}_{train}$ and σ^2_{train} are the global based feature sample mean and sample variance over the genuine training set, respectively, and α is a coefficient defining the threshold.

An alternative would be to consider a feature vector containing all the global based features. The natural extention to the multivariable case of the decision rule in Algorithm 1 would be Algorithm 2 in Fig. 2 (right). There, $\mathbf{g}_{test}$ denotes the global based feature vector corresponding to the test signature, $\overline{\mathbf{g}}_{train}$ and Σ_{train} are the global based feature vector sample mean and sample covariance over the genuine training set, respectively, and α is a coefficient defining the threshold. The decision rule means that signatures whose feature vectors lie outside the hyperellipsoid defined as $(\mathbf{g}_{test} - \overline{\mathbf{g}}_{train})^T \Sigma^{-1}_{train} (\mathbf{g}_{test} - \overline{\mathbf{g}}_{train}) = \alpha^2$ are considered as forgeries. Figure 2 (left) illustrates this for the case of a 2-dimensional feature vector.

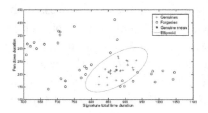

Algorithm 2

If $(g_{test} - \overline{g}_{train})^T \Sigma^{-1}_{train} (g_{test} - \overline{g}_{train}) > \alpha^2$

   then signature=FORGERY

   else continue classification

Fig. 2. Left: Distribution of the global feature vectors for the genuine and forged signatures of an author in the database. In this case, the feature vector is composed by the signature total time duration and the pen down duration. Right: Decision rule.

Coefficient α^2 is computed, for the global based feature vector, in three different ways for comparison purposes, namely, as: *i.* the maximum, or *ii.* the mean, or *iii.* the minimum, over all the authors in the Training Set of the database, of the maximum, over all the signatures of each author, of the positive definite quantity (note the reader that this is the so-called Mahalanobis distance):

$$d(\mathbf{g}_{test}, \overline{\mathbf{g}}_{train}) = (\mathbf{g}_{test} - \overline{\mathbf{g}}_{train})^T \Sigma^{-1}_{train} (\mathbf{g}_{test} - \overline{\mathbf{g}}_{train}). \tag{1}$$

That is (for case i.),

$$\alpha^2 = \max_{A} \max_{A_i} \left\{ (\mathbf{g}_{test} - \overline{\mathbf{g}}_{train})^T \Sigma^{-1}_{train} (\mathbf{g}_{test} - \overline{\mathbf{g}}_{train}) \right\}, \tag{2}$$

where A is the set of all the authors in the Training Set and A_i denotes the i-th author in the same set.

For the univariate case in Algorithm 1, equation (2) becomes:

$$\alpha^2 = \max_{A} \max_{A_i} \left\{ \frac{\left| g_{test} - \overline{g}_{train} \right|^2}{\sigma^2_{train}} \right\}. \tag{3}$$

A different approach, where only the signature total time has been used for pre-classification purposes, has been proposed by Lee and colleagues.[7] There, the threshold is computed as a fraction of the $\overline{g}_{train}$, and it is heuristically set to 0.2.

3. Feature Extraction

Typically, the measured data consists of three discrete time functions: pen coordinates x and y, and pressure p. In addition, several extended functions can be computed from them.[4,9] Previous to the feature extraction, the original pen coordinates are normalized regarding scale and translation.

3.1. *Global based features*

Several global based features can be extracted from the measured and extended time functions. These features should be selected to be discriminative enough in order for the proposed pre-classification to be succesful. The following global based features, corresponding to the better ranked ones by feature selection performed in the literature,[4,5] are used in this paper: signature total time duration T, pen down duration T_{pd}, positive x velocity duration T_{vx}, average pressure $\overline{P}$, maximum pressure P_M and the time at which the pressure is maximum T_{PM}.

3.2. *Time function based features*

Several extended time functions can be computed from the measured ones. In this paper, the path velocity magnitude v_T, the path-tangent angle θ, the total acceleration a_T and the log curvature radius ρ are computed.[9] The set is then composed by x, y, p, v_T, θ, a_T and ρ, and their first and second order time derivatives.

A wavelet approximation of the time functions is proposed to model them. The Discrete Wavelet Transform (DWT) decomposes the signal at different resolution levels, splitting it in low (*approximation*) and high (*details*) frequency components. The idea here is to use the DWT approximation coefficients to represent the time functions. Resampling of the time functions, previous to the DWT decomposition, is needed in order to have a fixed-length feature vector. To use a fixed-length feature vector represents an advantage since it makes the comparison between two signatures easier. A fixed-length representation based on Legendre Polynomials series expansions has been introduced by the present authors.[10] The approximation accuracy is determined by the chosen resolution level, which also determines the length of the resulting feature vector. Since this length has to be kept reasonably small, there will be a trade-off between accuracy and feature vector length. The design parameter is then the length of the feature vector, which determines the resolution level to be used. The widely used **db4** wavelets[11] is employed for the representation of the time functions.

4. Evaluation Protocol

The SigComp2011 Dataset[12] is used for the verification experiments. It has two separate datasets, containing Western (Dutch) and Chinese signatures, respectively. Each dataset, is divided into a Training and a Testing Set. Skilled forgeries (in which forgers are allowed to practice the reference signature for as long as they deem it necessary) are available. The signatures were acquired using a ballpoint pen on paper over a WACOM Tablet, which is the natural writing process. The measured data are the pen coordinates x and y, and pressure p.

For each dataset, the optimization of the meta-parameters of the system is performed over the corresponding Training Set while the Testing Set is used for independent testing purposes. The meta-parameters are: α for the pre-classification stage, the normalized length of the resampled time functions, the resolution level for the wavelet approximations, and the number of trees and randomly selected splitting variables for the RF classifier. To obtain statistically significant results, a 5-fold cross-validation (5-fold CV) is performed over the Testing Set to estimate the verification errors. For each instance of the 5-fold CV, a signature of a particular writer from one of the testing sets in the 5-fold CV is fed to the system. After its preprocessing, the global based features ($\mathbf{g}_{test}$) are extracted from it. Then, the pre-classification is performed as follows: the distance in (1) between $\mathbf{g}_{test}$ and $\overline{\mathbf{g}}_{train}$ (sample mean computed over the current writer's genuine signatures available in the training set of the 5-fold CV) is computed. If this distance is larger than the threshold (α^2), the signature is declared to be a forgery. If this is not the case, the signature is subjected to the subsequent classification stage, as follows: the DWT approximation coefficients are computed for the different time funtions being considered. Then, a RF classifier is trained by the current writer's genuine class in the training set of the 5-fold CV, and a forged class consisting of the genuine signatures of all the remaining writers in the same set. The result of the verification process is then either the result of the pre-classification (the input signature is considered a forgery), or the result of the RF classifier. If the result is given by the pre-classification, the verification process is speeded up.

To evaluate the performance, the EER (Equal Error Rate) is calculated, using the Bosaris toolkit,[13] from the Detection Error TradeOff (DET) Curve as the point in the curve where the FRR (False Rejection Rate) equals the FAR (False Acceptance Rate). The cost of the log-likelihood ratios[14] C_{llr} and its minimal possible value C_{llrmin} are also computed using the toolkit. A smaller value of C_{llrmin} indicates a better system performance.

5. Results and Discussion

To evaluate the individual discriminative power of the global based features, experiments using each one of them separately for pre-classification purposes were carried out. The results are presented in Subsec. 5.1. On the other hand, experiments using all the global based features in a combined feature vector for pre-classification were also carried out. The correlation between the individual global based features is taken into account through the global based feature vector covariance. This is important, since the features are not likely to be independent. The results are presented in Subsec. 5.2. In both cases, the experiments were performed using 500 trees and $\sqrt{P}$ randomly selected splitting variables ($P =$ feature vector dimension), for the RF classifier. The time functions were resampled to a normalized length of 256. The wavelet resolution level was set to 3, in order to obtain a feature vector of a reasonable length.

M. Parodi and J. C. Gómez

5.1. *Univariate case*

The verification results, with pre-classification, for the six global based features considered, and the three different values of α, are shown in Table 1, for the Dutch (left) and Chinese (right) data. The best results are indicated in **boldfaced** style. For comparison purposes, also the results without pre-classification are included in the last row section of Table 1. Results based on Legendre polynomials representations (without pre-classification),[10] are also included in that section.

Table 1. Verification results for the Dutch (left) and Chinese (right) Datasets.

	Dutch Dataset						Chinese Dataset					
	T	T_{pd}	T_{vx}	$\bar{P}$	P_M	T_{PM}	T	T_{pd}	T_{vx}	$\bar{P}$	P_M	T_{PM}
						α_{max}						
EER	5.35	6.22	4.95	4.93	6.58	7.08	5.65	7.64	7.01	7.05	7.84	7.91
$\bar{c}_{llr}$	0.237	0.238	0.228	0.212	0.254	0.270	0.224	0.301	0.264	0.263	0.291	0.284
$\bar{c}_{llrmin}$	0.201	0.205	**0.160**	0.168	0.214	0.240	0.193	0.253	0.218	0.215	0.243	0.251
						α_{mean}						
EER	5.98	6.61	6.64	6.01	8.17	8.91	4.93	7.63	6.88	6.92	8.42	8.85
$\bar{c}_{llr}$	0.256	0.272	0.260	0.255	0.301	0.303	0.200	0.293	0.274	0.271	0.321	0.333
$\bar{c}_{llrmin}$	0.226	0.241	0.241	0.227	0.276	0.284	**0.178**	0.250	0.228	0.231	0.283	0.286
						α_{min}						
EER	14.94	15.91	13.24	10.63	11.83	10.20	11.40	14.80	10.47	10.22	12.67	12.16
$\bar{c}_{llr}$	0.388	0.440	0.383	0.348	0.408	0.338	0.333	0.453	0.338	0.333	0.427	0.384
$\bar{c}_{llrmin}$	0.382	0.424	0.365	0.335	0.399	0.323	0.318	0.414	0.311	0.314	0.387	0.358
	Without pre-class			Previous results[10]			Without pre-class			Previous results[10]		
EER	6.78			5.91			7.90			10.03		
$\bar{c}_{llr}$	0.249			0.237			0.312			0.360		
$\bar{c}_{llrmin}$	0.205			0.195			0.247			0.296		

From Table 1, it can be seen that the proposed pre-classification does improve the error rates with respect to the case of not using it. This is not the case for every value of α. The actual values of α belong to the intervals: $[3,4]$, $[2,3]$ and $[1,2]$, for the *max*, the *mean* and the *min* criteria, respectively. The maximum α defines a conservative threshold, while α_{min} allows for more signatures to be pre-classified at the cost of larger errors (in the sense of classifying genuine signatures as forgeries). Then, α_{mean} is a trade-off value of α. The results confirm this, since using α_{max} leads, in most of the cases, to better results than using α_{mean}, while using α_{min} leads to the worst results. For the Dutch data, the error rates improve only when using α_{max}. This shows that many genuine signatures are beyond $2\sigma_{gen}$. For the Chinese data, the error rates are still improved when using α_{mean}, achieving the best error rate in this case. For this data, the threshold can be chosen to be a more robust one.

The pre-classifications based on P_M, T_{PM} and T_{pd} did not get any error rate improvements. In the cases of P_M and T_{PM}, this seems to be reasonable. The time at which the pressure is maximum T_{PM} is probably an unstable feature, since people is not likely to be consistent in the time where the pen pressure reaches a peak. The value of P_M, is likely to be dependant on the writing surface, the pen, etc., making it hard to make pre-classification decisions based only on this feature. On the other hand, in the case of T_{pd}, the result was unexpected, since it is believed that forgers are not able to accurately reproduce the pen down time of the genuine writers. The global based features used for pre-classification, leading to error rate improvements, were: T, T_{vx} and $\bar{P}$. In the case of T, the results confirm the well known fact that this feature is a good discriminator[7]. The value of $\bar{P}$, is likely to be more consistent than the other pressure based features, since people may not make considerable changes in the average pressure when signing. Finally, T_{vx} proved to have a high discriminative power, since it is probable that forgers may go back (*i.e.*, negative x velocity) several times during the writing process.

The best error rates were achieved using α_{max} and T_{vx}, and using α_{mean} and T, for the Dutch and Chinese data, respectively. For the Chinese data, the result is not surprising since T is a highly discriminative feature. For the Dutch data, the result could be explained considering that, in most of the cases, horizontal traces are more significant than vertical ones. Then, differences in the time in which the writer is writing forward would indicate that a forged signing process is taking place.

5.2. *Multivariate case*

Three different ways of computing α are described in Sec. 2 for the multivariate case. For the univariate case discussed above, the results using α_{max} are, in most of the cases, better than those using α_{mean}, while using α_{min} leads to the worst results. This is also the case for the multivariate case analized here. Moreover, in this case, the results using α_{mean} and α_{min} are not good, and for this reason they are not shown here. The verification results, with the pre-classification performed based on the feature vector combining all the considered global based features for $\alpha^2{}_{max}$, are shown in Table 2, for the Dutch (left) and Chinese (right) data, respectively. The best results are indicated in **boldfaced** style.

Table 2. Verification results for the Dutch and Chinese Datasets.

		Dutch Dataset		Chinese Dataset	
	EER	11.23		13.01	
$\alpha^2{}_{max}$	C_{llr}	0.3046		0.3533	
	C_{llrmin}	0.2978		0.3494	
	EER	3.09		4.99	
$\lambda\alpha^2{}_{max}$	C_{llr}	0.1589		0.2173	
	C_{llrmin}	**0.1123**		**0.1696**	
System		Commercial	1st non-comm.	Commercial	1st non-comm.
C_{llr}		0.2589	0.4928	0.4134	0.5651
C_{llrmin}		0.1226	0.2375	0.2179	0.3511

The results obtained with $\alpha^2{}_{max}$ shown in Table 2 are not good. This is an unexpected result, since it would be reasonable to expect that increasing the feature space dimensionality would increase the signatures separability. Figure 3 shows an example of the distribution of feature vectors composed by the signature total time duration and the pen down duration for the genuine and forged signatures of an author in the Training Set. Of course, this is a two-dimensional simplification of the multivariate case proposed here where the six global based features are combined into a feature vector. Nevertheless, Fig. 3 can be used to illustrate the idea that combining the global based features increases the discriminative power. The ellipsoid in solid line in Fig. 3 is the one defined by $\alpha^2{}_{max}$ computed resorting to (2). Note that, even though α_{max} is being used, there are genuine signatures that lie outside this ellipsoid which will be wrongly classified as forgeries. This is probably due to the fact that α is always computed over a separate set of genuine signatures used exclusively for training purposes, without taking into account the forgeries which are also available in the Training Set. However, it is clear from Fig. 3 that it is possible to enlarge the ellipsoid in such a way that less genuine signatures lie outside it so that the results can be improved. Figure 3, where a larger ellipsoid containing the original one has been plotted in dashed line, illustrates this. Then, by redefining the threshold (multiplying α^2_{max} by a factor $\lambda > 1$) a better result can be obtained.

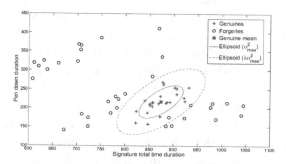

Fig. 3. Distribution of the global feature vectors (composed by the signature total time duration and the pen down duration) for the genuine and forged signatures of an author in the Training Set.

It is important to note that the genuine and forged signatures are, in general, more overlapped when the global based features are considered individually than when they are combined in a unique feature vector. Note that, if the dimensionality of the feature vectors in Fig. 3 is reduced (by projecting them to one axis), the corresponding representations of the genuine and forged signatures will not be easily separable. The results obtained when applying each of the three α criteria will differ in the amount of genuine signatures that will be wrongly classified as forgeries but, it will not be possible, with only one feature, to avoid misclassifications. Multiplying α by a factor (as proposed for the multivariate case) will not make any improvements, since the two classes are strongly overlapped. For this reason, the proposed threshold can not be easily modified to improve the results (as in the multivariate case). On the other hand, for the multivariate case, genuine and forged signatures are not that overlapped. Then, the fact that some genuine signatures are being missclassified is not due to the overlapping of the classes but to the threshold definition. Note that, the proposed redefinition of the threshold only makes sense in the multivariate case.

The verification results, for the multivariate case and the redefined threshold $\lambda\alpha^2_{max}$, are also shown in Table 2. Parameter λ was optimized over the Training Set, its value being equal to 5 for the Dutch and equal to 4 for the Chinese signatures. These results show that the new threshold leads to improvements with respect to the case of using α^2_{max}. The results also show improvements with respect to the cases where no pre-classification is performed (last row section in Table 1).

The results in the multivariate case outperform the best ones in the univariate case. This confirms that the global based features have a high discriminative power when they are combined. Note that, the increment in the signatures separability due to the increment of the feature space dimensionality, is only possible if the selected global based features are discriminative enough. This is the case here since the global based features used correspond to the better ranked ones among several commonly used global based features.[4,5] If this were not the case, increasing the feature space dimensionality would not necessarily improve the results.

For comparison purposes, the results for the best commercial and non-commercial systems in Sig-Comp2011[12] are included in the last row section of Table 2. Note, from Tables 1 and 2 that, even for the univariate case, the best results are comparable to those in the state-of-the-art. Moreover, the results for the multivariate case outperform those in the state-of-the-art.

In addition, the pre-classification helps to simplify and speed up the verification process. In Fig. 4, the percentage of the pre-classified signatures out of the total amount, for each of the three α criteria (univariate case), and both thresholds α^2_{max} and $\lambda\alpha^2_{max}$ (multivariate case), are shown for the Dutch (right) and Chinese (left) data, respectively. Note that, still in the most conservative cases (α_{max} for the univariate and $\lambda\alpha^2_{max}$ for the multivariate cases), an important part of the whole set of signatures is discarded making the system to further process less signatures. In particular, 40% and 25% of the Chinese and Dutch data, respectively, for the univariate case, and 55% and 30% of the Chinese and Dutch data, respectively, for the multivariate case, are discarded.

6. Conclusions

A pre-classification approach based on global based features, was proposed for an online signature verification system. The approach proved to be capable of exploiting the discriminative power of the global based features to improve the overall performance with respect to the case where no pre-classification is carried out. In addition, the obtained results are comparable to the ones of the state-of-the-art. The method has the advantage of being very simple, since it is based only on global based features, but proved to be powerful, allowing significant improvements in verification errors, process speed and simplicity of the whole signature verification system.

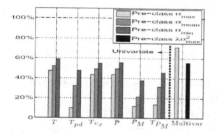 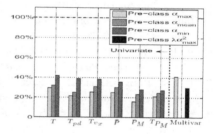

Fig. 4. Percentage of signatures pre-classified as forgeries, using the different thresholds.

Experiments using each one of the global based features separately to perform the pre-classification were carried out to evaluate their individual discriminative power. The total signature time duration, the pen down duration and the average pressure showed to be discriminative enough so that when used for pre-classification the obtained verification results outperform the ones obtained when no pre-classification is performed. Experiments combining the global based features in a unique feature vector, taking into account their correlation, were also carried out. The verification results obtained in this case outperform the ones obtained when using the features individually. This was expected since, being the features discriminative enough, an increment in the feature space dimensionality is likely to improve the separability between genuine and forged signatures.

References

1. M. Parodi and J.C. Gómez, Online Signature Verification: Improving Performance through Pre-classification Based on Global Features, *in LNCS*, Springer, Vol. 8158, pp. 69–76 (2013).
2. D. Impedovo and G. Pirlo, Automatic Signature Verification: The State of the Art, *IEEE Trans. on Syst., Man, and Cybern.-Part C: Applic. and Reviews*, 38(5), 609–635 (2008).
3. D. Maramatsu and T. Matsumoto, Effectiveness of Pen Pressure, Azimuth, and Altitude Features for Online Signature Verification, *in Proc. of Int. Conf. on Biomet.*, pp. 503–512 (2007).
4. J. Richiardi, H. Ketabdar, and A. Drygajlo, Local and Global Feature Selection for Online Signature Verification, *in Proc. of 8th ICDAR* (2005).
5. J. Fierrez-Aguilar, L. Nanni, J. Lopez-Peñalba, J. Ortega-Garcia, and D. Maltoni, An On-line Signature Verification System Based on Fusion of Local and Global Information, *in Proc. of IAPR Int. Conf. on Audio- and Video-Based Biomet. Person Auth.*, pp. 523–532 (2005).
6. R. Plamondon, The Design of an On-line Signature Verification System: From Theory to Practice, *Pattern Recognit. and Artif. Intell.*, 8(3), 795–811 (1994).
7. L. Lee, T. Berger, and E. Aviczer, Reliable on-line human signature verification systems, *IEEE Trans. on PAMI*, 18(6), 643–647 (1996).
8. L. Breiman, Random Forests, *Technical report*, U.C. Berkeley (2001).
9. J. Fierrez-Aguilar, J. Ortega-Garcia, D. Ramos-Castro, and J. Gonzalez-Rodriguez, HMM-based On-line Signature Verification: Feature Extraction and Signature Modelling, *Pattern Recognition Letters*, 28, 2325–2334 (2007).
10. M. Parodi, J.C. Gómez, and M. Liwicki, Online Signature Verification Based on Legendre Series Representation. Robustness Assessment of Different Feature Combinations, *in Proc. of 13th ICFHR*, pp. 377–382 (2012).
11. I. Daubechies, *Ten Lectures on Wavelets*, SIAM, Pennsylvania (1992).
12. M. Liwicki, M. Malik, C. den Heuvel, X. Chen, C. Berger, R. Stoel, M. Blumenstein, and B. Found, Signature verification competition for online and offline skilled forgeries (SigComp2011), *in Proc. of 11th ICDAR*, pp. 1480–1484 (2011).
13. N. Brümmer and J. du Preez, Application-independent Evaluation of Speaker Detection, *Comput. Speech & Language*, 20, 230–275 (2006).
14. D.R.J. Gonzalez-Rodriguez, J. Fierrez-Aguilar and J. Ortega-Garcia, Bayesian analysis of fingerprint, face and signature evidences with automatic biometric systems, *Forensic Science Int.*, 155, 126–140 (2005).

CHAPTER 5

INSTANCE SELECTION METHOD IN MULTI-EXPERT SYSTEM FOR ONLINE SIGNATURE VERIFICATION

Giuseppe Pirlo[1], Donato Barbuzzi[1] and Donato Impedovo[2]

[1]*Department of Computer Science, Bari University*
Via E. Orabona, 4 - 70125 Bari, Italy
E-mail: {giuseppe.pirlo, donato.barbuzzi}@uniba.it

[2]*Department of Electrical and Electronic Engineering, Bari Polytechnic*
Via E. Orabona, 4 - 70125 Bari, Italy
E-mail: impedovo@deemail.poliba.it

In real world applications, signature verification systems should be able to learn continuously, as new signatures providing additional information become available. In fact, new data are not equally relevant for system improvement and a suitable data filtering strategy is generally required. In this context, instance selection is an important task for signature verification systems in order to select useful signatures to be considered for updating system knowledge, removing irrelevant and/or redundant instances from new data.

This paper proposes a new feedback-based learning strategy to update the knowledge-base in multi-expert signature verification system. In particular, the collective behavior of classifiers is considered to select the samples for updating system knowledge. Evaluation tests provide a comparison between our (not naïve) approach and the traditional approach, which uses the entire new dataset for feedback. For the purpose, two state-of-the-art classifiers (NB and k-NN) and two abstract level combination techniques (MV and WMV) were used. The experimental results, carried out considering the SUSig database, demonstrate the effectiveness of the new strategy.

1. Introduction

The recent years have been characterized by the growing interest toward personal identity authentication along with the spreading of the internet and the increased demand for security issues. In particular, between biometric traits, handwritten signature is one of the most widespread means for personal authentication. In fact, many institutions recognize signatures as a legal means of verifying an individual's identity. In addition, signature verification is a non-invasive biometric technique, and people are familiar with using the signatures for identity verification in their everyday life.[1,2,3,4,5,6]

Different categories of signature verification systems are generally considered: offline and online systems. In offline verification systems only the signature image is available. In online verification systems temporal and spatial information of each stroke of the signature is available.[7]

Online verification systems are gaining more and more interest since dynamic information makes signatures more difficult to forge. Therefore, it can be expected that online systems would be more reliable than offline ones. In addition, electronic pen-input devices — like tablets and PDAs — are gaining popularity for signature acquisition in several daily applications.

When online systems are considered, researchers have long argued about the effectiveness of the different time functions available[1,2,8] and regional distribution of information[9,10,11] for signature verification.

Figure 1[12] sketches the three main phases of automatic signature verification: data acquisition and preprocessing, feature extraction and classification. During enrolment phase, the input signatures are processed and their personal features are extracted and stored into knowledge base. During the classification phase, personal features extracted from an inputted signature are compared against the information in the knowledge base, in order to judge the authenticity of the inputted signature.

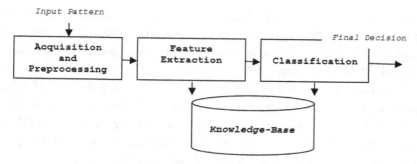

Fig. 1. Process of signature verification.

However the problems such as accuracy improvement and reduction of required size for training sample are still open. The characteristic of an individual's signature can only be established using an appropriate set of updated signature specimens, since human signature could significantly vary over time.

In order to solve these problems this paper proposes a multi-expert parallel system[13,14] that verifies the possibility to learn from the collective behavior of the whole set of classifiers, as new data becomes available. In particular the problem of selecting specific samples in order to update the knowledge base of each single classifier is addressed and compared against standard approach in which the entire set of new training samples is feed to each classifier.[15–19]

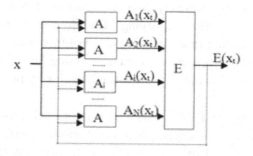

Fig. 2. Feedback in the multi-expert parallel system.

For this purpose, the feedback parallel topology in Fig. 2 is considered and experimental tests are carried out in the field of signature verification on the SUSig database, considering different types of features. Two different combination techniques (Majority Vote and Weighted Majority Vote) and two different state-of-the-art classifiers (NB and k-NN) have been used.

The experimental results demonstrate, in terms of reduction of false rejection rate (FRR) of genuine signatures and false acceptance rate (FAR) of forgery signatures, that a feedback strategy can be useful to improve the performance of the individual classifiers of a multi-expert system and, finally, to improve the performance of the whole system.

The paper is organized as follows. Section 2 presents a review of instance selection methods. Section 3 shows the operating conditions for test. The experimental results are presented in Section 4. Section 5 reports some discussions and the conclusion of the work.

2. Instance Selection Methods

2.1. *State of the art*

A pattern recognition system consists of two main processes: *enrollment* (or training) and *matching* (or recognition). In the enrollment phase, samples of specific classes are acquired, processed and features extracted. These features are labeled with the ground truth and used to generate the model representing the class. The matching phase performs the recognition of the (unknown) input pattern by comparing it against the enrolled templates. However, several instances stored in the training set can be not useful for classifying. Therefore it is possible to get acceptable classification rates ignoring non useful cases. This process is known as *instance selection*. Of course, training set reduction allows reducing runtimes in the classification and/or training stages of classifiers.

Given a training set T, the goal of an instance selection method is to obtain a subset $S \subset T$ such that S does not contain superfluous instances and $Acc(S) \sim = Acc(T)$ where $Acc(X)$ is the classification accuracy obtained using X as training set (henceforth, S is used to denote the selected subset). Instance selection methods can either start with $S = \emptyset$ (incremental method) or $S = T$ (decremental method). The difference is that the incremental methods include instances in S during the selection process and decremental methods remove instances from S along the selection.

Like in feature selection, according to the strategy used for selecting instances, we can divide the instance selection methods in two groups:[20]

— *Wrapper.* The selection criterion is based on the accuracy obtained by a classifier (commonly, those instances that do not contribute with the classification accuracy are discarded from the training set).

— *Filter.* The selection criterion uses a selection function which is not based on a classifier.

Based on the results reported in the literature about instance selection[20], among the wrapper methods based on the k-NN rule, the best options for selecting instances are DROP3 and GCNN since they have good performance in both accuracy and retention. While in filter methods, where the selection criterion is not based on a classifier, some approaches are focused on selecting border instances, among them, POC-NN, OSC and PSR have good performance, reaching with the selected subset, acceptable accuracy rates when different classifiers are used. Filter methods are competitive with the wrapper in both accuracy and retention and, as an additional characteristic, filter methods are faster than wrapper when medium/large datasets are processed.

In the next paragraph a new strategy is depicted taking into account a multi-expert system that works in supervised learning.

2.2. *Selecting instances in multi-expert system*

Let be:

- C_j, for $j = 1,2,...,M$, the set of pattern classes;
- $P = \{x_k \mid k = 1,2,..., K\}$, a set of pattern to be feed to the Multi Expert (ME) system. P is considered to be partitioned into S subsets P_1, P_2, ..., P_s, ..., P_S, being $P_s = \{x_k \in P \mid k \in [N_s \cdot (s-1)+1, N_s \cdot s]\}$ and $N_s = K/S$ (N_s integer), that are fed to the multi-expert system. In particular, P_1 is used for learning only, whereas $P_2, P_3,...,P_s,...,P_S$ are used both for classification and learning (when necessary);

- $y_s \in \Omega$, the label for the x_s pattern, $\Omega = \{C_1, C_2, ..., C_M\}$;
- A_i the i-th classifier for $i = 1, 2, ..., N$;
- $F_i(k) = (F_{i,1}(k), F_{i,2}(k), ..., F_{i,r}(k), ..., F_{i,R}(k))$ the feature vector used by A_i for representing the pattern $x_k \in P$ (for the sake of simplicity it is here assumed that each classifier uses R real values as features);
- $KB_i(k)$, the knowledge base of A_i after the processing of P_k. In particular $KB_i(k) = (KB_i^1(k), KB_i^2(k), ..., KB_i^M(k))$;
- E the multi expert system which combines H_i hypothesis in order to obtain the final one.

In first stage ($s = 1$), the classifier A_i is trained using the patterns $x_k \in P_i^* = P_1$. Therefore, the knowledge base $KB_i(s)$ of A_i is initially defined as:

$$KB_i(s) = (KB^1_i(s), KB^2_i(s), ..., KB^j_i(s), ..., KB^M_i(s)) \tag{1a}$$

where, for $j = 1, 2, ..., M$:

$$KB^j_i(s) = (F^j_{i,1}(s), F^j_{i,2}(s), ..., F^j_{i,r}(s), ..., F^j_{i,R}(s)) \tag{1b}$$

being $F^j_{i,r}(s)$ the set of the r-th feature of the i-th classifier for the patterns of the class C_j that belongs to P_i^*.

Successively, the subsets $P_2, P_3, ..., P_s, ..., P_S$ is provided to the multi-classifier system both for classification and for learning. The "leave-one-out" method is used to test the multi-expert system. When considering new labeled data (samples of $P_2, P_3, ..., P_s, ..., P_S$), a naïve and not naïve strategy can be used.

The naïve strategy uses all the available new patterns to update the knowledge base of each individual classifier:

- $\forall x_t \in P_s : update\_KB_i$ (2)

The second approach is derived from AdaBoost and bagging. A_i is updated by considering all its samples correctly recognized by ME system:

- $\forall x_t \in P_s \; \exists'(E(x_t) = y_t) : update\_KB_i$ (3)

In order to inspect and take advantage of the common behavior of the ensemble of classifiers, the following simple strategy is evaluated and compared to the previous.

3. Operating Conditions

3.1. *Classifiers and combination techniques*

The classifiers used for the experimentation are: Naïve Bayes Classifier and k-Nearest Neighbor. The first fits, in the training phase, a multivariate normal density to each class C_j considering a diagonal covariance matrix. Given an input to be classified, the Maximum a Posteriori (MAP) decision rule is adopted to select the most probable hypothesis among the different classes. The second is a very simple classifier which is also very easy to be updated with new patterns. The classification accuracy is influenced by the number of nearest neighbors k. Results reported in this work have been obtained by k = 3.

Finally, in this work the following decision combination techniques have been considered and compared: Majority Vote (MV) and Weighted Majority Vote (WMV). MV just considers labels provided by the individual classifiers, it is generally adopted if no knowledge is available about performance of classifiers so that they are equal-considered. The second approach can be adopted by considering weights related to the performance of individual classifiers on a specific dataset. Given the case depicted in this work, it seems to be more realistic, in fact the behavior of classifiers can be evaluated, for instance, on the training set. In particular, let ε_i be the error rate of the i-th classifier evaluated on the last available training set, the weight assigned to

$$A_i \text{ is, } w_i = \log(1/\beta_i) \text{ being } \beta_i = \varepsilon_i /(1 - \varepsilon_i) \tag{4}$$

3.2. *SUSig handwritten signature database*

The SUSig database consists of online signatures donated by 100 people (29 women and 71 men).[21] The database was collected in two separate

G. Pirlo, D. Barbuzzi and D. Impedovo

sessions that were approximately one week apart. Each person supplied 10 samples of his/her regular signature in each session, for a total of 20 genuine signatures, without any constraints on how to sign. Each person was then asked to forge a randomly selected user's signature. So, 10 forged signatures were produced.

Therefore, in our case a multi-expert system for on-line signature verification has been considered P={x_j | j=1,2,…,30} (classes "0" and "1") has been used. Figure 3 presents some samples of handwritten signatures.[21]

Fig. 3. Sample genuine signature from SUSig.

The DB has been initially partitioned into 2 subsets:

- $P_1 = \{x_1,…, x_8,x_{11},…,x_{18},x_{21},…,x_{28}\}$,
- $P_2 = \{x_9,x_{10},x_{19},x_{20},x_{29},x_{30}\}$.

In particular, P_1 represents the set usually adopted for training and test considering the "leave-one-out" method on SUSig DB.[21] P_2 is the feedback dataset. Each signature is partitioned into 5 strokes, successively, for each stroke, the following set of features has been considered:

— F_1: feature set 1: mean and variance of the distances between two consecutive points;
— F_2: feature set 2: mean and variance of pressure between two consecutive points;
— F_3: feature set 3: mean and variance of the velocity and acceleration between two consecutive points.

4. Experimental Results

This section presents the results in terms of false rejection rate (FRR) of genuine signatures and the false acceptance rate (FAR) of forgery signatures. We combined, adopting a multi-expert system, the three set of features (F1, F2 and F3) and two classifiers: NB and k-NN. The label "X-feed" refers to the use of the X modality for the feedback training process: "All" is the feedback of the entire set. "MV" and "WMV" are feedback at ME level adopting, respectively, the majority vote and the weighted majority vote schema.

First successful results, related to the use of NB classifier with weighted majority vote and majority vote as combination techniques, have already been discussed in a previous paper.[22] While Table 1 shows results related to the use of k-NN (k = 3) classifier and majority vote as combination technique. P1 is used for training and test in "leave-one-out" approach and P2 is used for feedback learning. The first column (No-feed) reports results related to the use of P1 for training and test, without applying any feedback (0 Selected Samples), while the approach All-feed uses all samples belonging to the new set in order to update the knowledge base of each single classifier (All Selected Samples).

Table 1. 3-NN, MV Combination Technique, Feedback — P_2.

	No-feed	MV-feed	All-feed
FAR	14.30	10.74	12.18
FRR	4.65	4.06	5.11

For MV-feed an improvement both of the FAR is 1.44% and of the FRR is 1.05% respect to the use of the entire new dataset.

Finally, Table 2 shows results related to the use of same classifier and weighted majority vote as combination technique. P1 is used for training and test in "leave-one-out" approach and P2 is used for feedback learning. In this case, for WMV-feed the improvement of the FAR is

0.86% and of the FRR is 0.86% compared to the use of the All-feed strategy where entire new dataset is used for the feedback.

Table 2. 3-NN, WMV Combination Technique, Feedback — P_2.

	No-feed	WMV-feed	All-feed
FAR	8.38	6.21	7.07
FRR	5.85	4.57	5.43

More specifically, these tables demonstrate that MV-feed and WMV-feed outperform each other feedback-based strategy.

5. Conclusion and Future Works

This paper provides a comparison between two approaches (naïve and not naïve) for retraining a multi-expert system for automatic signature verification. More specifically, our strategy (not naïve) that exploits the collective behavior of classifiers to select the most profitable samples for knowledge-base updating, outperforms other approaches when new signatures became available.

Finally, the experimental results demonstrate the collective behavior of a set of classifiers provides useful information to improve system performance, depending on the feature type and matching strategy. Future works will inspect the possibility of evaluate this approach with respect to the methods of instance selection presented in literature.

References

1. M. Parodi, J. C. Gòmez, M. Liwicki: Online Signature Verification Based on Legendre Series Representation. Robustness Assessment of Different Feature Combinations, Proc. XIII International Conference on Frontiers in Handwriting Recognition (ICFHR 2012), Monopoli, Bari, Italy, 18-20 Sept. 2012, pp.377–382.
2. D. Impedovo, G. Pirlo, R. Plamondon: Handwritten Signature Verification: New Advancements and Open Issues, Proc. XIII International Conference on Frontiers in Handwriting Recognition (ICFHR 2012), Monopoli, Bari, Italy, 18–20 Sept. 2012, pp. 365–370.
3. K. W. Boyer, V. Govindaraju, N. K. Ratha: Special issue on recent advances in biometric systems, *IEEE T-SMC — Part B*, vol. 37, no. 5, pp. 1091–1095, Oct. 2007.

4. S. Prabhakar, J. Kittler, D. Maltoni, L. O'Gorman, T. Tan: Special issue on biometrics: Progress and directions, IEEE T-PAMI, vol. 29, no. 4, pp. 513–516, Apr. 2007.
5. A. K. Jain, L. Hong, S. Pankanti: Biometric identification, Commun. ACM, vol. 43, no. 2, pp. 91–98, Feb. 2000.
6. A. K. Jain, P. Flynn, A. Ross: Handbook of Biometrics, NewYork: Springer-Verlag, 2007.
7. D. Yeung, H. Chang, Y. Xiong, S. George, R. Kashi, T. Matsumoto, G. Rigoll: "SVC2004: First international signature verification competition" in International Conference on Biometric Authentication, 2004, pp. 16–22.
8. K. Franke, S. Rose: Ink-deposition analysis using temporal data, in Proc. 10th Int. Workshop Front. Handwriting Recognition. (IWFHR), La Baule, France, 2006, pp. 447–453.
9. G. Pirlo, D. Impedovo: Fuzzy-Zoning-Based Classification for Handwritten Characters, *IEEE Trans. on Fuzzy Systems*, Vol. 19 , Issue 4, pp. 780–785, 2011.
10. S. Impedovo, A. Ferrante, R. Modugno, G. Pirlo: Feature Membership Functions in Voronoi-based Zoning, Proceedings of the 11th International Conference of the Italian Association for Artificial Intelligence, December 9-12, 2009, Reggio Emilia, Italy, LNAI, Vol. 5883, 2009, Springer Verlag, Germany, pp. 202–211.
11. S. Impedovo, R. Modugno, A. Ferrante, G. Pirlo: Zoning Methods for Hand-written Character Recognition: An Overview, Proceedings of the 12th International Conference on Frontiers in Handwriting Recognition (ICFHR-12), Nov. 16-18, 2010, Kolkata, India, IEEE Computer Society Press, pp. 329–334.
12. D. Impedovo, G. Pirlo: Automatic Signature Verification — State of the Art, IEEE Transactions on Systems, Man and Cybernetics — Part C: Applications and Review, vol. 38, no. 5, September 2008, pp. 609–635.
13. J. Kittler, M. Hatef, R.P.W. Duin, J. Matias: On combining classifiers, IEEE Trans. on PAMI, Vol.20, no.3, pp.226–239, 1998.
14. V. Di Lecce, G. Dimauro, A. Guerriero, S. Impedovo, G. Pirlo, A. Salzo: A Multi-expert System for Dynamic Signature Verification, in Multiple Classifier Systems, Series in Lecture Notes in Computer Science — Vol 1857, Ed. J. Kittler et al., Berlin, 2000, pp. 320–329.
15. D. Barbuzzi, D. Impedovo, G. Pirlo: Supervised Learning Strategies in Multi-Classifier Systems, Proc. 11th International Conference on Information Science, Signal Processing and their Applications (ISSPA 2012), Montreal, Canada, July 3–5, 2012, p. 1215–1220.
16. G. Pirlo, C.A. Trullo, D. Impedovo: A Feedback-based multi-classifier system, Proceedings of the 10th International Conference on Document Analysis and Recognition (ICDAR-10), July 26–29, 2009, Barcelona, Spain, IEEE Computer Society Press, pp. 713-717.
17. D. Impedovo, G. Pirlo: Updating Knowledge in Feedback-based Multi-Classifier Systems, in *Proc. of ICDAR*, pp. 227–231, 2011.
18. D. Barbuzzi, D. Impedovo, G. Pirlo: Feedback-Based Strategies In Multi-Expert Systems, In: Sesto Convegno del Gruppo Italiano Ricercatori in Pattern Recognition, 2012.
19. D. Barbuzzi, D. Impedovo, G. Pirlo: Benchmarking of Update Learning Strategies on Digit Classifier Systems. In: Proceedings of the 13th International Conference on Frontiers in Handwriting Recognition, 2012, pp. 35–40.

20. J. A. Olvera-López, J. A. Carrasco-Ochoa, J. F. Martínez-Trinidad, J. Kittler: A review of instance selection methods, Artificial Intelligence Review, vol. 32, Issue 2, August 2010, pp. 133–143.
21. A. Kholmatov, B. Yanikoglu: SUSIG: an on-line signature database, associated protocols and benchmark results, Pattern Analysis and Applications, pp. 1–10, 2008.
22. G. Pirlo, D. Impedovo, D. Barbuzzi: Learning Strategies for Knowledge-Base Updating in Online Signature Verification Systems. In: New Trends in Image Analysis and Processing — ICIAP 2013 (EAHSP - Emerging Aspects on Handwritten Signature Process). LECTURE NOTES IN COMPUTER SCIENCE, vol. 8158, p. 86–94.

CHAPTER 6

TOWARDS A SHARED CONCEPTUALIZATION FOR AUTOMATIC SIGNATURE VERIFICATION

Marcus Liwicki, Muhammad Imran Malik, and Charles Berger

German Research Center for Artificial Intelligence, Germany
E-mail: {firstname.lastname}@.dfki.de

Netherlands Forensic Institute, The Hague, the Netherlands
E-mail: charles.berger@.nfi.minvenj.nl

This chapter is an effort towards the development of a shared conceptualization regarding automatic signature verification especially between the Pattern Recognition (PR) and Forensic Handwriting Examiners (FHEs) communities. This is required because FHEs require state-of-the-art PR systems to incorporate them in forensic casework but so far most of these systems are not directly applicable to such environments. This is because of various differences, right from terminology to evaluation, in how the signature verification problem is approached in the two said communities. This chapter, therefore, addresses three major areas where the two communities differ and suggest possible solutions to their effect. First, it highlights how signature verification is taken differently in the above mentioned communities and why this gap is increasing. Various factors that widen this gap are discussed with reference to some of the recent signature verification studies and probable solutions are suggested. Second, it discusses the state-of-the-art evaluation and its problems as seen by FHEs. The real evaluation issues faced by FHEs, when trying to incorporate automatic signature verification systems in their routine casework, are presented. Third, it reports a standardized evaluation scheme capable of fulfilling the requirements of both PR researchers and FHEs and provides a practical exemplar of its usage.

1. Introduction

The research community is interested in signature verification since centuries. The technological revolution that came by the emergence of computers has shifted this interest towards automatic verification of signatures. Today, industry in general and FHEs in particular look forward for automatic signature verification. It will assist FHEs in performing their routine signature verification tasks efficiently and effectively. While there is an increasing demand of automatic systems in forensic handwriting examination departments, there are certain barriers/gaps between the two communities, i.e., PR community and FHEs community, starting from the terminology till the evaluation of outcomes. This chapter will highlight a few of the most important of these gaps and will suggest their probable solutions.

Note that forensic scenarios have some built-in complexities like signature samples taken from torn or muddy papers, clothes, etc., which are not considered here. We will focus on daily routine cases of FHEs, where signature samples are available similarly to PR research and yet FHEs find application of automatic signature verification systems nearly impossible. The specific problems addressed are non-accessible data sets and non-representative data, difference in terminology used by different PR researchers, the output reported by automatic systems and the current evaluation scheme. This chapter can be viewed as an effort to standardize the evaluation criteria for signature verification. The standardized criteria will be useful for both the PR researchers and FHEs. It is a similar effort as previously done in the field of image binarization.[1]

The rest of this chapter is organized as follows. In Section **2** signature verification is defined with respect to PR researchers. Section **3** defines signature verification with respect to FHEs. This is required to highlight the basic differences and similarities among the definitions of various modalities in the two communities. Section **4** makes the core of this chapter where we move towards standardization and highlight the most important barriers to the application of automatic systems in forensic departments. Each of these barriers is discussed and its probable solutions are suggested. A special attention is given to the third and the fourth barriers, i.e., the state-of-the-art output reporting and the state-of-the-art evaluation, respectively. Section **5** summarizes the chapter and suggests some future work.

2. Automatic Signature Verification: PR View

Today the PR community moves by defining the automatic signature verification as a two-class pattern classification problem.[2] Note that in earlier PR studies it was defined differently where PR researchers also considered other genres of signatures such as, disguised signatures.[3] As a two class classifier, an automated system has to decide whether or not a given signature belongs to a referenced authentic author. If a system could find enough evidence of genuine authorship from the questioned signature, it considers the signature as genuine; otherwise it declares the signature as forged. Note that in the PR community various types of forgeries are studied and in fact sometimes the same forgery type is termed differently by different researchers.[4] In the following we are only stating the most commonly reported forgery types by PR researchers.

(i) Random Forgery: genuine signature of any writer other than the authentic author.
(ii) Simple/Casual Forgery: the forger only knows the name of the authentic author.
(iii) Simulated Forgery: produced by inexperienced forger after practicing unrestricted number of times.
(iv) Skilled Forgery: produced by experienced forger, usually a calligrapher, after practicing unrestricted number of times.

Moreover, automated signature verification is divided into, online and offline, depending on the mode of the handwritten input. If both spatial and temporal information are available to a system, verification is performed on online data. In the case where temporal information is not available and a system can only utilize the spatial information gleaned through scanned or camera captured documents, verification is performed on offline data.[2]

3. Signature Verification: FHE View

FHEs view signature verification as a multi-class (more than two classes) classification.[5] It involves various genres of natural and unnatural handwriting. Due to space limitations, we will focus only on the main categories of signature types that are relevant to the discussion at hand.

(i)   Genuine Signatures: naturally written authentic signatures of the specimen author.
(ii) Disguised Signatures: '*not*' a forgery, but an authentic author imitates his/her own signature to make it look like a forgery so that it can be denied at a later time. Note that disguised signatures are a product an unnatural signing behavior, yet they are from the authentic author.
(iii) Simple Forgery: the forger knows the original signatures (seen for some time) and forges without practice. This is in contrast to the PR definition of simple forgery where a forger may only know the name of an authentic author.
(iv) Skilled Forgery: the forger knows the original signatures and forges after practicing unrestricted number of times.

FHEs take the terms simulated and forged in the same meaning.[6] The forgeries/simulations can either be made free hand or traced. Whether traced or free hand, they can be simple or skilled. Furthermore, note that the term "random forgery" does not appear here. This is because a random forgery, as defined by PR researchers, is considered as a fictitious case by FHEs and hence they usually do not consider it.[6]

4. Moving Towards Standardization: Bridging the Gaps

In the following section we highlight various gaps/barriers which must be considered for the development of a common understanding between the PR researchers and FHEs. These are,

(i)   Non-accessible datasets and non-representative data.
(ii) Different terminology and modalities/categories.

(iii) Output produced by the state-of-the-art systems.
(iv) State-of-the-art evaluation.

4.1. *Non-accessible datasets and non-representative data*

Many PR systems are not trained/tested on publicly available data and therefore the experiments are not repeatable/verifiable. Due to this the FHEs can never be sure of which systems can potentially be better applied to their casework. Furthermore, a majority of the state-of-the-art signature verification systems are built, tested, and optimized for data that are not a representative for data faced in forensic cases. These PR data usually contain various fictitious signatures, like "random forgeries" as discussed above.

Probable solution

To bridge this gap the PR researchers should use data that are publicly available preferably collected by FHEs in forensic like situations. Today a large amount of such data are publicly available, such as the data from various signature verification competitions jointly organized by PR researchers and FHEs. These include SigComp2009,[7] 4NSigComp2010,[5] SigComp2011,[8] and 4NSigComp2012.[9] All of these datasets are publicly available at the International Association of Pattern Recognition (IAPR), Technical Committee (TC-11) webpage[i]. Having different automated systems that report results on the same data sets may provide a comparative analysis of their performances.

If application specific data are collected for special purposes they should be unbiased and have statistical significance. Moreover the following information is at least required.

(i) Details about data collection procedures applied to acquire the data.
(ii) Any specific restrictions applied while collection, any errors occurred and corrective measures taken.
(iii) When and if the data will be publicly available.

4.2. *Different terminology and modalities/categories*

In PR researchers and FHEs define some of the signature verification modalities/categories differently, e.g., the term *Simple Forgery* (refer to the Sections **2** and **3**). Moreover, different PR researchers sometimes give the same name to different signature modalities. Some examples of such mismatch include Refs.[10-12]

In addition to that, in some cases a lot of PR research reveals results that are trivial/irrelevant with respect to forensic casework, e.g., a common practice of PR researchers is to report random forgeries but they are fictitious in view of forensic experts. If random forgeries are included in a test set while evaluating the results of a system, a system having very low error rate may still not be suitable for forensic casework. On the other hand a system having a high error rate but considering skilled forgeries may yield better results in forensic casework. Examples are reported in Table 1. Note that, these examples are from PR literature and are presented here just to highlight the difficulty FHEs face when viewing these results where different types of signature modalities are either differently defined or in some cases are combined with each other while reporting the overall system performance. As given in Table 1, System[13] and System[14] are producing higher error rates with skilled and simulated forgeries than other systems which either do not specify the types of forgeries considered, e.g., System[10] and System[11], or do not use forgeries in evaluation like System[15] and System.[16] Viewing these results an FHE cannot say anything with certainty about which system will perform better in real forensic casework. However System[13] and System[14] are reporting their results on skilled forgeries separately thereby giving hints to the potential performance of these systems in forensic casework.

Probable solution

Settling down on common definition would favor the application of automatic systems in real forensic casework.[6] It is suggested here that the two communities may use the following terms.

- Genuine: for authentic signatures.
- Forged: for simulated signatures.

Table 1. Results of some recent signature verification systems.

System	Database	FAR (%)	FRR (%)
Ref. 10	320(G), 320(F), 640(T)	0.11	0.02
Ref. 11	300(G), 300(F), 600(T)	4.16	7.51
Ref. 13	980(G),980(F), 1960(T)	0.01(RF), 4.29(SF), 19.80(SK)	2.04
Ref. 14	300(G), 600(F), 900(T)	4.41(RF), 1.67(SF), 15.67(SM)	10.33
Ref. 15	2400(G), 0(F), 2400(T)	0.64	1.17
Ref. 16	500(G), 0(F), 500(T)	9.81	3

F = Forgery, G = Genuine Signature, RF = Random forgery, SF = Simple forgery, SK = Skilled forgery, SM = Simulated forgery, and T = Total number of signatures.

- Simple forgery: a forgery where actual signatures are known but forgery is produced without any practice.
- Skilled forgery: same as simple forgery but produced after practice.

We emphasize that the term "random forgery" should not be used anymore since it refers to fictitious or random signatures. If such fictitious signatures are used for some specific training purposes, they must be separated from the actual forgery types and should not affect the overall evaluation. Moreover, other types of signing behaviors as studied by FHEs, e.g., disguised signatures, should be focused by PR researchers.

The datasets of 4NSigComp2010 and 4NSigComp2012 (available on the IAPR TC-11 datasets webpage) can be used for this purpose.

4.3. *Output by the state-of-the-art systems*

What should an automated signature verification system output in order to be successfully applicable in forensic casework? This is a substantial question for both PR researchers and FHEs.

The output produced usually by automated systems is not acceptable for presentation in the courts thereby making the use of automatic systems nearly impossible for FHEs.[8] Traditionally, automated signature verification systems report their decisions in a Boolean manner, i.e., if enough evidence of a forgery is present, a system reports a reject, otherwise an accept. Though this is quite objective and may be significant in some fields like real time application, e.g., banking, but a Boolean answer of *genuine* otherwise *forged* is not adequate for the FHEs. They are interested to exactly know how close a questioned signature to a genuine signature is when it is declared as forged and vice versa.

To bridge this gap, automated systems usually provide some sort of similarity score between 0 and 1, e.g., probability values. Here a value near 0 represents a forgery and a value near 1 represents genuine authorship. This again is inadequate for forensic casework because mere scores/probability values in themselves raise many questions for FHEs and courts: how are these values related to the authorship (genuine or forged) and among themselves; how to compare different systems producing different values for the same questioned signature; how would an FHE establish that a value of 0.2 produced by one automated system is still more close of being genuine signature than a value of 0.4 produced by another system; how would these sort of outputs be defended in courts?

Moreover, FHEs are interested to know the features contributing to the output. They would like to consider the features' uniqueness/rarity in a population, e.g., how rare is the style of writing a special character in a population? This information impacts the overall evaluation of an FHE while examining a signature sample. But how would that relate to an automated system?

Probable solution

A probable solution is that the automated systems should produce some continuous similarity/difference score's' (that may vary between any two extremes like, '0.001' to '1000') which would be converted into evidential value/Likelihood Ratios (LR) according to the Bayesian approach.[17]

The overall idea of this solution is given in Fig. 1. Here the score's' is computed by comparison between the questioned signature and the reference signatures. In addition to that the different source comparison is performed by considering the signatures of all other authors available in the training set. The same source comparison is also performed if

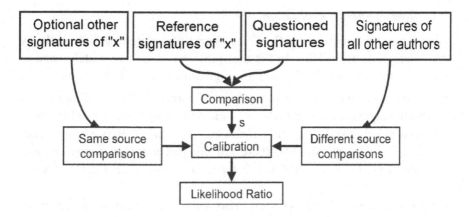

Fig. 1. An overview of evaluation scheme.

other signatures of the referenced author are available. The scores can be converted into LRs by a so-called calibration procedure,[18] such as the one implemented in the FoCal toolkit[ii]. The LR is actually the ratio of the probabilities of finding that score's's' when questioned signature is genuine and when it is forged. Such LR values are supposed to suffice the needs of FHEs especially when considering the features' rarity in a population.

Note that so-far the computation of some kind of likelihood ratios has been realized in different ways only in some tools and frameworks, such as CEDAR-FOX,[19,20] and WANDA project,[21] but in general the PR community has not adopted the likelihood ratios at large. This makes the application of the majority of state-of-the-art PR methods impossible in forensic casework.

Furthermore, PR researchers are sometimes not interested in continuous values like likelihood ratios. They usually demand an objective indicators of a system's performance. In the next section we will first explain the state-of-the-art of PR evaluation. Then suggest how the above mentioned likelihood ratios may be converted to depict an objective measure to suit the needs of PR researchers at the same time.

4.4. *State-of-the-art evaluation*

The results of signature verification systems are evaluated differently by PR researchers and FHEs. In PR the following terms are widely used to report on the evaluation of automatic signature verification systems.[22]

- Accuracy: measures the percentage of correctly classified signatures with respect to all signatures under investigation. 22 When only accuracy is used, a system that votes by chance may show higher accuracy if, for example, there are unequal number of genuine and forged signatures in a dataset. To rectify this, often FRR and FAR are considered.

- False Rejection Rate (FRR): Also known as '*miss probability*' or *Type-I error*. It is the rate at which genuine signatures are classified as forged by a system.

- False Acceptance Rate (FAR): Also known as *false alarm probability* or *Type II error*. It is the rate at which forged signatures are classified as genuine by a system. Both FRR and FAR are usually given in percentage.

- Receiver Operating Characteristic (ROC) curve: FRR and FAR can be computed at any given threshold but in order to view the complete behavior of a signature verification system a ROC-curve is often plotted. This curve represents FRR and FAR at all possible thresholds for a system (as an alternative, the FAR could also be plotted against True Accept Rate (TAR)).

- Area Under Curve (AUC): It represents the probability that a system gives higher value to a randomly chosen genuine signature as compared to a randomly chosen forgery. As the name suggests, the smaller the area under ROC-curve, the better is a system's performance.

- Equal Error Rate (EER): The point on the ROC-curve where FRR equals FAR.

- Average Error Rate (AER): It is the mean of FRR and FAR. Usually used when no decision threshold can be adjusted, e.g., on a final test set when trying to assess the performance without adjusting any parameter.

- Detection Error Trade-off (DET) curve: It is a variant of the ROC curve that is plotted using mapping according to the Probit function.

The current state-of-the-art of evaluation, as given above, is not adequate for FHEs. In many circumstances an FHE reports a continuous measure of evidential value to the court. In fact an FHE is included in a judicial investigation to facilitate the court by analyzing handwritten text/signatures and reporting the evidence of a forgery or genuine authorship. The court does not demand a decision from an FHE, rather a continuous measure of similarity or difference. This is because a pure classification, as done in PR, cannot be combined with other circumstantial evidence, e.g., opportunity, motive, fingerprints, etc. in a legally acceptable way.

Since the current evaluation methods primarily evaluate performance on the basis of correct or wrong classification they are inadequate to fulfill the needs of FHEs. Therefore, we need an alternative evaluation scheme that would serve the following two purposes.

- First, fulfill the demands of FHEs and enable them present the results of automated systems in courts.
- Second, objective enough so that to enable PR researchers compare the performance of their systems in an objective/direct manner preferably also representable as a single score.

Probable solution: Standardized performance evaluation scheme

As suggested previously, automatic signature verification systems should output continuous scores that can be converted into LRs or Log LRs (LLRs) by various calibration procedures. These conversions need to be monotonic thereby not affecting the discrimination between the genuine and forged signatures as suggested by an automated system. After these conversions, the signatures having weak evidence of forgery generally do not lead to high absolute values of LRs, while the signatures with a strong evidence of forgery lead to high absolute values of LRs.

We have already tested this evaluation scheme and applied it successfully in the SigComp2011, 4NSigComp2012, and SigWiComp2013 signature verification competitions. Table 2 shows

Table 2. Results for Dutch off-line signature verification from SigWiComp2013.

ID	Accuracy (%)	FRR (%)	FAR (%)	$\hat{C}_{llr}$	$\hat{C}^{min}_{llr}$
1	67.90	31.90	32.14	2.00	0.90
2	**76.90**	**23.70**	**23.10**	**0.90**	**0.64**
3	75.60	24.44	24.44	1.08	0.70
4	74.93	25.20	25.10	0.98	0.70
5	73.80	26.70	26.20	3.94	0.73
6	72.14	27.41	27.93	0.97	0.74
7	70.90	29.63	29.10	1.10	0.78
8	69.16	31.11	30.80	1.02	0.74
9	70.15	29.63	29.90	1.10	0.74
10	72.95	27.41	27	1.02	0.72

Note: Winner was declared on the basis of the minimum value of $\left(\hat{C}^{min}_{llr}\right)$.

some of the results received on the Dutch offline dataset in SigWiComp2013 signature verification and writer identification competition. Note that this evaluation scheme suggests the PR researchers to report results in the form of LLRs and their corresponding cost $(\hat{C}_{llr})$. The LLR would help FHEs in presenting the results of automated systems in the judicial courts. Furthermore, $(\hat{C}^{min}_{llr})$ is calculated which is the minimum possible value of $(\hat{C}_{llr})$ and can be calculated as suggested by Bruemmer.[18] This $(\hat{C}^{min}_{llr})$ value can be used as a final assessment score of a system's performance in PR research.

As depicted in Table 2, the system with the best FRR and FAR also has the best value of $(\hat{C}^{min}_{llr})$, i.e., minimum value. But, from here we cannot generalize that a system having better FRR and FAR will always have better $(\hat{C}^{min}_{llr})$. It is obvious from the results, that a good EER does not always result in a good $(\hat{C}^{min}_{llr})$, e.g., in Table 2 System 3 performs better than System 4 when looking at the EER, but the $(\hat{C}^{min}_{llr})$ of System 4 is better than that of System 3. This might be explained by the fact that a few large errors might spoil the overall performance with $(\hat{C}^{min}_{llr})$. Similar is the case with the Systems 9 and 8 on the same task. This is an important observation as it gives a clue that the evaluation metric used in this competition, i.e., $(\hat{C}^{min}_{llr})$, not only looks into the number of errors but is also influenced by the severity of respective errors. This makes the $(\hat{C}^{min}_{llr})$ well suited for forensic applications where considering severity

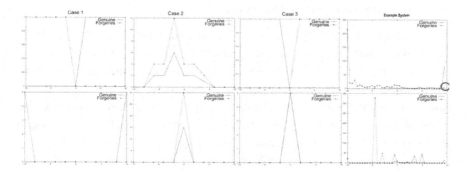

Fig. 2. LLR curves before (on top) and after calibration (on bottom), possible extreme cases (Case 1 to Case 3), and results of a real system (a wrong classification–marked with a green circle–affected the overall results on $(\hat{C}_{llr})$ thereby increasing the $(\hat{C}^{min}_{llr})$ value for this system). X-axis: (Optimized) Log Likelihood, Y-axis: No. of Occurrences.

of errors is substantial as a severely mistaken system (although may be having a very low EER) may lead a person to death.

To further clarify, three extreme cases that can occur while following this scheme in evaluation are presented in Fig. 2. The distributions of the LLRs of genuine signatures (target values) and forgeries (non-target values) are depicted in red lines and blue dotted lines, respectively. These distributions can be interpreted as follows. The curves on the top represent the non-calibrated evidential values, while the respective curves on the bottom are produced after calibrating with the Focal tool kit. The farther the tar-curve goes to the left, the higher would be the cost of this misleading decision. Similarly, the farther the nontar-curve goes to the right, the higher would be the cost. For optimal performance and thereby for the minimum value of $(\hat{C}^{min}_{llr})$, the two curves must be optimally separated. In Case 1 the curves are perfectly separated and lay on their desired sides. Therefore, the calibrated LLRs have the minimum cost, thus the $(\hat{C}^{min}_{llr})$ will be equal to 0. Cases 2 and 3 present a perfectly non-distinguishing and an always misclassifying system, respectively. In both of these cases, the $(\hat{C}^{min}_{llr})$ will be equal to 1 that is the maximum cost. As a reference, the LLR curves for a real system are also given in Fig. 2 on the right side. Note that as there is a wrong classification with a high LLR (marked with a green circle), and it affects the overall results thereby increasing the $(\hat{C}^{min}_{llr})$ value for this system.

5. Summary and Future Directions

In this chapter the points of view of the two communities, PR and FHEs, regarding about signature verification are discussed. We have presented various barriers/issues that hinder the application of automatic signature verification systems in real forensic casework and have proposed solutions to that effect. We believe that by adopting these solutions, the state-of-the-art signature verification methods will find ample opportunities for direct applications in real forensic casework.

In the future it is hoped that both the PR and FHE communities would move together to further enhance the scope of their collaborative work. PR experts are encouraged to develop system also targeting the needs of FHEs. In the meanwhile FHEs are encouraged to use more and more automated systems in their everyday casework and provide feedback to PR researchers. This is substantial since improvements in the current systems are only possible if they are exposed to tackle rigorous real world signature verification scenarios. Furthermore, FHEs should make more forensically relevant data publicly available. This will be a first step towards a common goal by the two communities, i.e., the application of automated systems in assisting FHEs while solving real forensic handwriting analysis cases.

Acknowledgments

We would like to acknowledge the various forensic handwriting examiners from Netherlands Forensic Institute and experts from the PR-community who have helped us while compiling this chapter.

References

1. Elisa H. Barney. Smith, 'An analysis of binarization ground truthing' in *DAS*, pp. 27–34, (2010).
2. D. Impedovo and G. Pirlo, 'Automatic signature verification: The state of the art', in *IEEE Transactions on Systems, Man, and Cybernetics, Part C (Applications and Reviews)*. 38(5), pp. 609–635, (2008).
3. R. Plamondon and G. Lorette, 'Automatic signature verification and writer identification — the state of the art', in *Pattern Recognition* 22, pp. 107–131, (1989).

4.   M. I. Malik and M. Liwicki. 'From terminology to evaluation: Performance assessment of automatic signature verification systems' in *ICFHR*, pp. 613–618, (2012).

5.   M. Liwicki, C. E. van den Heuvel, B. Found, and M. I. Malik, 'Forensic signature verification competition 4NSigComp2010 - detection of simulated and disguised signatures' in *ICFHR*, pp. 715–720, (2010).

6.   M. Liwicki, M. Blumenstein, B. Found, C. E. van den Heuvel, C. Berger, and R. Stoel, Eds. *Int. Workshop on Automated Forensic Handwriting Analysis*, vol. 768, (2011).

7.   V. L. Blankers, C. E. van den Heuvel, K. Y. Franke, and L. G. Vuurpijl, 'ICDAR 2009 signature verification competition' in *ICDAR*, pp. 1403–1407, (2009).

8.   M. Liwicki, M. I. Malik, C. E. van den Heuvel, X. Chen, C. Berger, R. Stoel, M. Blumenstein, and B. Found, 'Signature verification competition for online and offline skilled forgeries SigComp2011' in *ICDAR*, pp. 1480–1484, (2011).

9.   M. Liwicki, M. I. Malik, L. Alewijnse, C. E. van den Heuvel, and B. Found, 'ICFHR 2012 competition on automatic forensic signature verification (4NSigComp2012)' in *ICFHR*, pp. 823–828, (2012).

10. E. Ozgunduz, T. Senturk, and M. E. Karsligil, 'Off-line signature verification and recognition by support vector machines' in *EUSIPCO*, (2005).

11. S. Kumar, K. B. Raja, R. K. Chhotaray, and S. Pattanaik, 'Off-line signature verification based on fusion of grid and global features using neural networks', in *Int. Journal of Engineering Science and Technology* 2, pp. 7035–7044, (2010).

12. E. Justino, E. J. R. Justino, F. Bortolozzi, and R. Sabourin, 'Off-line signature verification using HMM for random, simple and skilled forgeries' in *ICDAR*, pp. 1031–1034, (2001).

13. L. Cordella, P. Foggia, C. Sansone, F. Tortorella, and M. Vento, 'A cascaded multiple expert system for verification' in *Multiple Classifier Systems, 1857, LNCS*, pp. 330–339, (2000).

14. C. Santos, E. J. R. Justino, F. Bortolozzi, and R. Sabourin, 'An off-line signature verification method based on the questioned document expert's approach and a neural network classifier' in *IWFHR*, pp. 498–502, (2004).

15. A. El-yacoubi, E. J. R. Justino, R. Sabourin, and F. Bortolozzi, 'Off-line signature verification using HMMs and cross-validation' in *IEEE Workshop on Neural Networks for Signal Processing*, pp. 859–868, (2000).

16. H. Baltzakis and N. Papamarkos, 'A new signature verification technique based on a two-stage neural network classifier', *Engineering Applications of Artificial Intelligence* 14(1), pp. 95–103 (2001).

17. J. Gonzalez-Rodriguez, J. Fierrez-Aguilar, D. Ramos-Castro, and J. Ortega Garcia, 'Bayesian analysis of fingerprint, face and signature evidences with automatic biometric systems', in *Forensic Science Int.* 155(2-3), pp. 126–140, (2005).

18. N. Bruemmer and J. du Preez, 'Application-independent evaluation of speaker detection' in *Computer Speech & Language* 20(2-3), pp. 230–275, (2006).

19. S. N. Srihari, B. Zhang, C. Tomai, S. Lee, Z. Shi, and Y. C. Shin, 'A system for handwriting matching and recognition' in *Symposium on Document Image Understanding Technology*, pp. 67–75, (2003).

20. R. J. Verduijn, C. E. van den Heuvel, and R. D. Stoel, Forensic requirements for automated handwriting analysis systems' in *IGS*, pp. 132–135, (2011).

21. K. Franke, L. Schomaker, C. Veenhuis, L. Vuurpijl, and I. Erp, M. van Guyon, 'WANDA: A common ground for forensic handwriting examination and writer identification', in *ENFHEX News*. pp. 23–47, (2004).
22. T. Fawcett, 'An introduction to ROC analysis', in *Pattern Recogn. Lett.* 27, pp. 861–874 (2006).

---

[i] http://www.iapr-tc11.org/mediawiki/index.php/Datasets_List
[ii] http://focaltoolkit.googlepages.com

CHAPTER 7

OFFLINE SIGNATURE VERIFICATION BASED ON PROBABILISTIC REPRESENTATION OF GRID EVENTS

Konstantina Barkoula[1], Elias N. Zois[2], Evangelos Zervas[2], George Economou[1]

[1]*Physics Department, University of Patras, Patras, 26500, Greece.*
E-mail: kbarkoula@gmail.com, economou@upatras.gr

[2]*Department of Electronics Engineering, Technological & Educational Institution of Athens, 12210, Egaleo, Greece.*
E-mail: {ezois, ezervas}@teiath.gr

A new grid based feature extraction methodology for offline handwritten signature representation is proposed which combines notions of grid feature extraction, set operations and information theory. It mutates the informative content of a set of binary mask elements (originally used to exploit the distribution formed by the transitions of signature pixels) by considering them as probabilistic events, simple or compound. Epigrammatically the feature definition procedure initiates by declaring an F_D-partition from a set of sixteen basic grid masks. In order to avoid exhaustive search among a huge number of possible F_D-partitions this work focuses on F_{4SR}-partitions of evenly distributed and orthogonal tetrads. All subset elements of an F_4- partition, considered as unique alphabet events that a discrete space source transmits when it is overlaid upon the signature image, are utilized as features and their distribution, as extracted by their mapping on the grid based binary signature image constitutes the novel proposed signature representation. Numerous ways of exploiting the entropy measure of the events distribution have been carried out in order to select the most appropriate scheme per writer. Results derived on two datasets indicate enhanced EER rates when compared to various state of the art approaches found in the literature.

1. Introduction

In an era dominated by all forms of digital information the handwritten signature still continues to serve as an accepted trait for individuals to validate their identity in several application areas. The operation of the signing process is usually twofold. On the one hand, it is a way to provide evidence of deliberative consent of a writer by signing at the bottom of a document. On the other hand it can be used as a way to proclaim the writers presence and uniqueness.[1]

An immense anthology of research papers and broad reviews provide the basic principles that an Automated Signature Verification System (ASVS) follows.[2,3] In short, it is an ensemble of algorithms mainly from the research areas of image processing and pattern recognition. Both online and offline ASVS have to confront the fact that the motoric process and the intention of the writer during the signature generation phase are subject to natural variations which are described under the term *inter-writer variability*.[1,4] Offline feature extraction is one of the most challenging tasks when ASVS are designed. A growing feature extraction philosophy models the signature by applying either a coarse or a fine grid onto the image.[5–11] Then, signature representation are derived by appropriately modeling accumulated signature's image grid feature distributions. It is important to note that the informative content of the grid features depends on its coarseness or fineness.

The principal endeavor of this work is to advance the background concepts of a grid based feature which exploits signature pixel transition distributions[12] by mutating and evolving its descriptive and informative content. In order to do so, the union set operation is used for creating the feature extracting masks by mapping to images the powerset of grid subset members. This novel approach not only models the feature generation process as a discrete space random source accompanied by its probabilities but in addition it allows the use of information theory concepts, like entropy, in order to characterize its behavior.[13] Further, during the training phase of the verification stage, the selection of the most appropriate subset grid collection per signer is examined through the evaluation of a number of ad-hoc entropy selection algorithms. The verification results have been reported with the use of the GPDS and a proprietary database by utilizing the EER. The remaining of the work is divided as follows: Section 2 provide the preprocessing stage and the proposed feature extraction method. Section 3 describes the verification protocol and provides experimental results obtained using common protocols of the literature. Section 4 as a final point, provides the conclusions.

2. Feature Extraction

2.1. *Preprocessing*

The image preprocessing procedure is composed of the following steps: thresholding, skeletonization, cropping and segmentation. Thresholding is carried out using the Otsu's method.[14] Next, the skeleton of the signature is isolated by applying the corresponding morphological operation in an attempt to filter as much as possible unwanted noise originating from the device characteristics, i.e. the variability of the writing instrument. The experimental procedure has indicated that if the one pixel wide thinning algorithm is employed then there is a reduction of the informative content of the feature components which affects the discriminative power of it. In this way, the skeletonization process generates signature traces with more than one pixel wide, usually ranging from three up to five. The resulted image bounding rectangle and its corresponding Most Informative Window (MIW) is evaluated[12] followed by the segmentation procedure which relies on the ideas of equimass sampling grids.[15] This approach provides grid rectangles with equal amount of black pixels when compared to the trivial equidistant grid segmentation which provides segments of equal image area (see Fig. 1). The cropped signature image is initially segmented horizontally into strips of equal mass and then each strip is segmented vertically into equal mass rectangles, with no restriction for a grid segmentation, i.e. boundary lines being in the same vertical position for each horizontal strip (see Fig. 1). The segmentation procedure is adaptable to various segmentation $\{i \times j\}$ levels like 1x1-the full MIW, 2 x 2-the most usable one or the 3 x 3-(see Fig. 1).

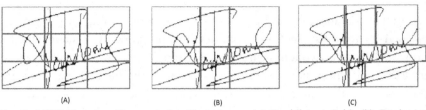

(A)   (B)   (C)

Fig. 1. MIW Signature Segmentation Techniques. (a) Equidistant Grid. (b) Equimass Grid (c) Equimass Rectangular. In this work the equimass rectangular selection has been applied in order to extract portions of signature with equal mass.

In order to illustrate the probabilistic nature of the proposed feature it is essential to describe the generation of the grid masks which will overlay on each part of the MIW image according to the selected segment scenarios.

2.2. Short mathematical background

Let the set $X \equiv F_{CB2} = \{G_i\}$, $i = 1{:}16$ to be defined as the collection of the binary image pixel path components of a 5 x 5 grid composed of three successive pixels while keeping the constraints of a) having the first and third pixels restrained to a Chebyshev distance equal to two and b) skimping paths which are symmetric[12] (see Fig. 2). As more than one G_i elements may coexist concurrently within the 5×5 overlay grid at a certain image position, it looks natural to extract information both from single as well as compound events from the $\{G_i\}$ masks. The number of both single and compound events from the elements of a set with cardinality $|X|$ is equal to $2^{|X|}$, which leads to a very high feature dimensionality. In order to reduce it, the functional and convenient concept of set partition is applied. The management of compound events of the subsets, defined by the partitioning of X, appears to be a more realistic approach.

A partition F_D of a set X is defined as a collection of D-disjoint subsets which satisfies the property that every element of X lies in exactly one of these subsets.[16] This work, for the sake of sanity, investigates the case in which the F_4 partition (a partition which contains a four subset collection) is utilized for feature extraction. In order to cope with the colossal amount[17] of potential ensembles of the F_4 partition family only a small number of them shall be utilized. Thus, further reduction in the total number of questioned F_4 partitions is accomplished by applying a two stage reduction method. Firstly, from the entire number of possible F_4 partitions the F_{4S} family of symmetric partitions has been secluded by selecting those which represent full symmetry in both the number of samples and the number of subsets. That is the F_{4S} partition is composed from four subsets, denoted by the index *ts,* of four elements each.

Additionally, further reduction to the 1820 F_{4S} possible partitions is achieved by requiring that the elements of a partition subset must comply with the orthogonality principle. The term orthogonal denotes that each element which is a member of a subspace of a F_{4S} partition cannot be expressed as a combination of the remaining three elements of the same subset. The complete set of all the possible ensembles of the newly formed F_{4SR} collection contains only 87 cases, hereafter denoted as *schemes* $SC^x_{4SR} = \{G^x_{4SR,ts}\}, x = 1...87, ts = \{1,2,3,4\}$, (see Fig. 2).

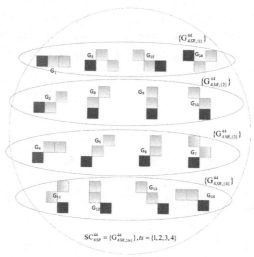

Fig. 2. One characteristic orthogonal partition of the F_{4SR} collection-partition. The total number of the orthogonal F_{4SR} partitions equals 87. The four partition subsets of the illustrated F_{4SR} collection are members of the $SC^{44}_{4SR} = \{G^{44}_{4SR,\{ts\}}\}$, $ts = \{1,2,3,4\}$ scheme: $SC^{44}_{4SR} = \{\{ G^{44}_{4SR,\{1\}} \}, \{ G^{44}_{4SR,\{2\}} \}, \{ G^{44}_{4SR,\{3\}} \}, \{ G^{44}_{4SR,\{4\}} \} \} = \{\{G_1, G_3, G_{15}, G_{16}\}, \{G_2, G_8, G_9, G_{10}\}, \{G_4, G_5, G_6, G_7\}, \{G_{11}, G_{12}, G_{13}, G_{14}\}\}$.

2.3. *Proposed representation*

Let a set Y be defined by its elements $Y = \{y_i\}, i = 1, .., N$. Then, a collection of subsets Σ which satisfies a number of desirable properties regarding non-emptiness as well as closure under complementation and countable unions is called a Σ-algebra.[16] Any Σ-algebra of a set lies between two limits: the first is the trivial set which consists of the empty set and the set itself only $\{\varnothing, Y\}$. The second is the powerset $2^{|Y|}$ which is the set of all subsets of Y including the set Y and the empty set.

Each of the subsets $G^x_{4SR,\{ps\}}$ of any given scheme SC^x_{4SR} can now be considered to play the role of the set $Y \equiv \{y_i\} \equiv \{G^x_{4SR,\{ts\}}\}$. The four element subsets of a SC^x_{4SR} scheme are used by means of their respective sixteen dimensional power-sets $2^{|Y|}$. For example, the $2^{|\{G_1, G_3, G_{15}, G_{16}\}|}$ powerset of the $Y \equiv \{G^{44}_{4SR,\{1\}}\}$ subset is composed of the following group of subsets: $\{\varnothing$, $\{G_1\}$, $\{G_3\}$, $\{G_{15}\}$, $\{G_{16}\}$, $\{G_1, G_3\}$, $\{G_1, G_{15}\}$, $\{G_1, G_{16}\}$, $\{G_3, G_{15}\}$, $\{G_3, G_{16}\}$, $\{G_{15}, G_{16}\}$, $\{G_1, G_3, G_{15}\}$, $\{G_1, G_3, G_{16}\}$, $\{G_1, G_{15}, G_{16}\}$, $\{G_3, G_{15}, G_{16}\}$, $\{G_1, G_3, G_{15}, G_{16}\}\}$. In order to define the final grid masks which will be used to acquire and extract the signature features a mapping from the powerset of a $G^x_{4SR,\{ts\}}$ subset to the corresponding grid image extraction subset is required and realized by applying the union operation $G^x_{ijkl,\{ts\}}$ on each element of the powerset (see Fig. 3).

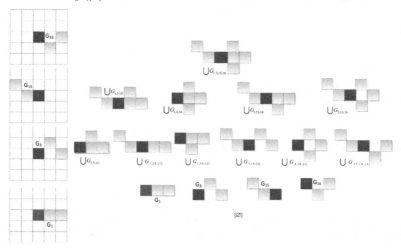

Fig. 3. The powerset of the subset $G^{44}_{4SR,\{1\}}$ of the SC^{44}_{4SR} scheme along with the corresponding grid image mappings.

Each scheme can be regarded to model the handwritten image-signature by its projection onto four, internally orthogonal, disjoint major subspaces (defined by their subsets).

The $\{ G^{x}_{4SR,\{ts\}} \}$ subsets further analyze the signature image by creating a 16 dimensional space with members the grid-structures of the formed probability space Ω. Overlaying of the 5×5 grid onto every signature image pixel can be viewed as a discrete space random source S where only one emitted simple or compound element or *event* is allowed to exist each time the grid sweeps the signature trace.

The entropy of source S is defined as it appears in eq. (1) where $p_S(\alpha)$, $a \in 2^{|Y|}$ is the distribution of the source elements $\{2^{|Y|}\}$. The final feature vector is denoted by $\{^{image\_segment}P_{scheme\#,subset\#}\} \equiv \{^{sg}P_{sc,ts}\}$ and composed from the corresponding probabilities of every mapped grid image. Its dimensionality is a linear function of the number of the signature segments.

$$^{sg}H_{sc,ts} = H(S) = -\sum_{a \in 2^{|Y|}} {^{sg}P_{sc,ts}(a)} \ln(^{sg}P_{sc,ts}(a)) \qquad (1)$$

3. Verification Procedure

The proposed signature representation has been evaluated in the context of writer dependent offline signature verification.[18] The authors have the belief that the writer dependent framework cannot support forensic cases with success due to the lack of highly skilled simulated samples. However it can be applicable to cases where simulated forgeries can be created for individuals like e.g. in financial transactions. The evaluation framework consists of three main stages:

(i)   Scheme (SC^{x}_{4SR}) selection per segment using the genuine signatures reference set per signer for signature representation,

(ii) Classifier training using signature representations of the reference set per signer.

(iii) Testing of the rest of the signature samples representations per signer. The evaluation is based on the Equal Error Rate (EER) which is expressed as a function of a global threshold per database.

The reference samples are chosen randomly and the remaining of the signature samples per signer are used for testing. The verification procedure is repeated a number of times so that the reported results present statistical significance. The selection of an appropriate SC_{4SR}^x scheme that will be used for signature feature extraction per segment is examined through several alternative combinations that will be presented in the next section based on the entropy of symbol distributions

The evaluation process is applied on two offline grey-scale signature databases: a proprietary Greek signers' database[12] composed of 105 genuine and 21 skilled forgery signature samples for 69 signers (CORPUS 1) and GPDS-300[5] composed of 24 genuine and 30 skilled forgery signature samples for 300 signers (CORPUS-2).

3.1. *Protocol*

Initially, *nref* reference genuine and *nref* reference skilled forgery signature samples are randomly selected per signer. The impact of the number of reference samples on the verification results is investigated by using two different numbers of reference samples, *nref* = 5 and *nref* = 12. The same random set of reference samples is used under different alternative experimental schemes for fair comparison.

In the current evaluation framework, signature's features are extracted both out of the whole signature's preprocessed image, as well as its 2×2 equimass rectangular segmentation. This segmentation captures both global and local features and is analogous to the '2×2' segmentation level[12] for comparison. Next, the representative SC_{4SR}^x scheme per image segment for each person is selected using the genuine reference signatures based on entropy criteria that will be exposed in the subsequent paragraph. Using the representative SC_{4SR}^x scheme for the writer, the signature's features are extracted.

The reference set signatures' representations are the input samples for classifier training. The trained classifier is a hard-margin Support Vector Machine (SVM) with a radial basis function (rbf) kernel using quadratic programming for optimization. Several rbf sigma values are examined for tuning purposes. The verifications rates as expressed by the EER reported are valid for a proper range of rbf sigma values. During testing, the rest of the genuine and skilled forgery signature samples representations are classified using the trained SVM classifier. The score "distance" of each test sample from the separating hyperplane of the SVM classifier, is utilized for EER calculation.

3.2. *Representative scheme selection based on entropy*

Given that the underlying feature is a probability distribution of symbols, the entropy of each distribution is a worthy candidate for defining the representative scheme selection criterion. The entropy measure as defined in information theory is the measure of uncertainty. In the context of the proposed representation, higher entropy values for the symbols of a tetrad scheme provide evidence about the uniformity of their distribution. This can be interpreted as an effective *fit* of the *ts*-tetrad to the symbolic content of the represented segment. In an opposite view, a lower entropy value could reveal a highly repetitive habit of the writer. So, the rest of this work conducts an investigation for selecting the most appropriate scheme for signature representation by enabling primitive order statistics on entropies.

Since four $\{G_{4SR,\{ts\}}^{x}\}$ subsets are available for each $SC_{4SR}^{x}, x \in \{1..87\}$ scheme there are several methods for evaluating entropies per segment and per writer. This procedure is mathematically presented by the following set of relations: First, the entropy value per *ts*-tetrad is evaluated by summing all the *i-indexed nref* samples:

$$^{sg}H_{sc,ts} = \sum_{i=1}^{nref} {}^{sg}H_{i,sc,ts} \tag{2}$$

Next, groups of entropy values per scheme are evaluated by applying primitive order statistics and mean values to eq. (2) entropies:

$$^{sg}H_{sc}^{min} = \min_{ts=1..4}\{{}^{sg}H_{sc,ts}\}$$

$$^{sg}H_{sc}^{max} = \max_{ts=1..4}\{{}^{sg}H_{sc,ts}\}$$

$$^{sg}H_{sc}^{med} = median_{ts=1..4}\{{}^{sg}H_{sc,ts}\} \tag{3}$$

$$^{sg}H_{sc}^{mean} = 0.25 \times \sum_{ts=1}^{4} {}^{sg}H_{sc,ts}$$

Finally, the most appropriate-representative scheme per segment and writer is declared by selecting the *appropriate asc-scheme* according to:

$$\begin{cases} {}^{sg}asc_{\min}^{\{\min,\max,med,mean\}} = \arg\min_{sc=1...87}\{{}^{sg}H_{sc}^{\{\min,\max,med,mean\}}\} \\ {}^{sg}asc_{\max}^{\{\min,\max,med,mean\}} = \arg\max_{sc=1...87}\{{}^{sg}H_{sc}^{\{\min,\max,med,mean\}}\} \end{cases} \tag{4}$$

3.3. Results and discussion

The verification process presented in the previous paragraphs is evaluated in configurations of either five (5) or twelve (12) reference samples from the genuine and skilled forgery class using both datasets. Since the experiments are repeated a number of times, the mean EER rates for the possible alternatives in selecting an *appropriate scheme*, as defined in relations (3) and (4), are presented (see Table 1). From the reported results (see Table 1) one can observe that the selection of the representative scheme per segment using the ${}^{sg}asc_{\min}^{\{\min\}}$ or ${}^{sg}asc_{\min}^{\{mean\}}$ approach results better when compared against the ${}^{sg}asc_{\max}^{\{\min\}}$ for both corpuses, both configurations of *nref* and all the alternatives defined in all the Eqs.(3) . This information naturally drives to the conclusion that the feature extraction procedure which corresponds to the ${}^{sg}asc_{\min}^{\{\min\}}$ F_{4SR} collection is the one that provides the most relevant information for verification since it reveals significant information about the repetitive habits of a writer. Finally, the EER values of this approach are compared against recently reported ones (see Table 2). From an inspection its is easily deduced that results are better or comparable to the results reported so far for the databases used in our experiments and similar reference sets.

Table 1. Mean EER (%) for both datasets (D1), (D2) and the alternative ways of asc-scheme selection. Results are provided for 5 and 12 training samples (5T, 12T cases).

	\multicolumn{8}{c}{Entropy values per scheme}							
	${}^{sg}H_{sc}^{\min}$		${}^{sg}H_{sc}^{\max}$		${}^{sg}H_{sc}^{\max}$		${}^{sg}H_{sc}^{\max}$	
asc-scheme	D1	D2	D1	D2	D1	D2	D1	D2
${}^{sg}asc_{\min}^{\{\}}$ (5T)	3.15	8.51	3.36	8.76	3.26	8.61	3.11	8.48
${}^{sg}asc_{\max}^{\{\}}$ (5T)	3.73	9.01	3.47	8.77	3.70	8.85	4.16	9.06
${}^{sg}asc_{\min}^{\{\}}$ (12T)	1.87	4.87	2.05	5.00	1.92	5.04	1.90	4.85
${}^{sg}asc_{\max}^{\{\}}$ (12T)	2.23	5.21	1.97	4.99	2.10	5.22	2.43	5.31

Note: The asc-scheme corresponds to the ${}^{sg}asc_{\min}^{\{\min,\max,med,mean\}}$ or the ${}^{sg}asc_{\max}^{\{\min,\max,med,mean\}}$.

Table 2. Comparison (EER) between this work and other recent research approaches.

# ref	D1		D2		Additional Comments
	5T	12T	5T	12T	
Proposed	3.11	1.87	8.48	4.85	-
From [12]	9.16	4.65	12.3	8.2	8.2: mean case *nref* = 10, 15
From [7]	—	—	12.0	—	GPDS-100
From [5]	—	—	—	9.0	100 writers
From [6]	*Writer Independent*			13.7	150 writers
From [10]	*Genuine only samples*			4.2	160 writers
From [19]	—	—	—	15.1	160 writers
From [20]	—	—	—	15.4	160 writers
From [21]	*Stability dependent*			4.0-5.4	300 writers

Note: 5T, 12T corresponds to training modes with 5 and 12 genuine samples.

4. Conclusions

The evolution of a grid based feature extraction method for off line signature modelling and verification has been demonstrated. It attempts to combine perceptions from the field of grid feature extraction, set operations and information theory. An entropy, order based investigation is provided in order to select the most appropriate verification schemes. Results derived from writer dependent protocols indicate that the presented method is comparable to state of the art techniques. The proposed method is expected to be enriched by a) waiving the symmetry property which will permit additional grid vectors b) providing additional sigma-algebra modeling and c) using writer independent verification protocols.

References

1. L. Alewijnse, "*Analysis of Signature Complexity*", Master Thesis, University of Amsterdam (2008).
2. F. Leclerc and R. Plamondon, "Automatic Signature Verification: The State of the Art: 1989-1993", *International Journal of Pattern Recognition and Artificial intelligence*, **8**, pp. 644–660 (1994).
3. D. Impedovo and G. Pirlo, "Automatic Signature Verification: The State of the Art", *IEEE Transactions on Systems Man and Cybernetics*, **38**, pp. 609–635 (2008).

4. M. C. Fairhurst, and E. Kaplani, "Perceptual Analysis of Handwritten Signatures for Biometric Authentication", *IEE Proceedings Vision, Image and Signal Processing*, **150**, pp.389–394 (2003).
5. J. F. Vargas, M. A. Ferrer, C. M. Travieso and J. B. Alonso, "Off-line Signature Verification Based on Grey Level Information Using Texture Features", *Pattern Recognition*, **44**, pp. 375–385 (2011).
6. R. Kumar, J. D. Sharma and B. Chanda, "Writer independent Off-Line Signature Verification Using Surroundedness Feature", *Pattern Recognition Letters*, **33**, pp. 301–308 (2012).
7. B. H. Shekar, and R. K. Bharathi, "LOG-Grid Based Off-Line Signature Verification", *Fourth International Conference on Signal and Image Processing 2012* Ed. S. Mohan, and S. S. Kumar, LNEE **222**, pp. 321–330 (Springer India, 2013).
8. J. P. Swanepoel, and J. Coester, "Off-Line Signature Verification Using Flexible Grid Features and Classifier Fusion", *International Conference on Frontiers in Handwriting Recognition*, (ICFHR 2012), pp. 297-302, (IEEE Press 2012).
9. A. Gilperez, F. Alonso-Fernandez, S. Pecharroman, J. Fierrez-Aguilar, and J. Ortega-Garcia, "Off-Line Signature Verification Using Contour Features", *International Conference on Frontiers in Handwriting Recognition*, pp. 1–6, (ICFHR 2008).
10. M. Parodi, J. C. Gomez, and A. Belaid, "A Circular Grid Based Rotation Invariant Feature Extraction Approach for Off-Line Signature Verification", *International Conference on Document Analysis and Recognition*, pp. 1289-1293, (IEEE Press 2011).
11. R. Wajid and A. B. Mansoor, "Classifier Performance Evaluation for Off-Line Signature Verification Using Local Binary Patterns", *European Workshop on Visual Information Processing*, pp. 250-254, (IEEE Press 2013).
12. K. Tselios, E. N. Zois, E. Siores, A. Nassiopoulos, and G. Economou, "Grid Based Feature Distributions for Off-Line Signature Verification", *IET Biometrics*, **1**, pp. 72–81 (2012).
13. T. M. Cover, and A. Y. Thomas, *Elements of Information Theory*, (John Wiley and Sons, 2006).
14. N. Otsu, "A Threshold Selection from Gray Level Histogram", *IEEE Transactions on Systems, Man and Cybernetics*, **6**, pp. 62–66 (1979).
15. J. Favata and G. Srikantan, "A Multiple Feature/Resolution Approach to Handprinted Digit and Character Recognition", *International Journal of Imaging Systems and Technology*, 7, pp. 304–311 (1996).
16. P. R. Halmos, *Naive Set Theory*, (Springer, 1960).
17. R. Gian-Carlo, "*The Number of Partitions of a Set*", American Mathematical Monthly, **71**, pp. 498–504 (1964).
18. L. Batista, D. Rivard, R. Sabourin, E. Granger, and P. Maupin, "State of the Art in Off-Line Signature Verification", *Pattern Recognition Technologies and*

Applications: Recent Advances Ed. B. Verma and M. Blumenstein, pp. 39–62 (2008).

19. V. Nguyen, Y. Kawazoe, T. Wakabayashi, U. Pal, and M. Blumenstein, "Performance Analysis of the Gradient Feature and the Modified Direction Feature for Off-Line Signature Verification", *International. Conference on Frontiers in Handwriting Recognition*, pp. 303–307 (IEEE press 2010).

20. M. B. Yilmaz, B. Yanikoglu, C. Tirkaz, and A. Kholmatov, "Off-Line Signature Verification Using Classifier Information of HOG and LBP Features", *International Joint Conference on Biometrics*, pp. 1–7 (IEEE press, 2011).

21. G. Pirlo and D. Impedovo, "Verification of Static Signature by Optical Flow Analysis", *IEEE Transactions on Human-Machine Systems*, **43**, pp. 499–505 (2013).

CHAPTER 8

LOCAL FEATURES FOR OFF-LINE
FORENSIC SIGNATURE VERIFICATION

Muhammad Imran Malik, Marcus Liwicki, and Andreas Dengel

German Research Center for Artificial Intelligence, Germany
E-mail: {firstname.lastname}@.dfki.de

University of Fribourg, Switzerland
E-mail: marcus.liwicki@.unifr.ch

The topic of signature verification has been addressed in the Pattern Recognition (PR) literature for several decades. The current PR research, at large, does not take the real needs of Forensic Handwriting Experts (FHEs) into account. The most crucial fact is that along with genuine and forged signatures, FHEs also have to deal with disguised signatures, i.e., when an author tries to make her/his own signatures look like a forgery. Our research in this area suggests that local or part-based features provide us a good possibility to identify disguising attempts. The purpose of this chapter is therefore twofold. First, we debate on the importance of disguised signatures with examples in order to draw the attention of PR community towards this important genre of signatures. Second, we present a novel comparison among three local features based off-line systems for forensic signature verification. The first system is a combination of scale-invariant Speeded Up Robust Features (SURF) and Fast Retina Keypoints (FREAK). The second system is based on a combination of Features from Accelerated Segment Test (FAST) and FREAK and the third system is based on nine local features with Gaussian Mixture Models (GMMs) classification. All of these systems are evaluated on the dataset of the 4NSigComp2010 signature verification competition which is the first publicly available dataset containing disguised signatures. Results indicate that our local features based systems

M. I. Malik, M. Liwicki and A. Dengel

outperform all the participants of the said competition both in terms of time and equal error rate.

1. Introduction

Signatures have been considered representative of human behavioral characteristics since centuries.[1,2] With the evolution of modern computing technologies, researchers have moved towards automatic verification of signatures. This shift has been reinforced by the interest various industries have in this field. One of the most important applications of automatic signature verification systems is in forensic science.[3]

Forensic signature verification in difficult cases, however, has until now been carried out without actual application of automated systems,[4] only a few tools like, Cedar-Fox,[5] Wanda,[6] and FISH,[7] are used by some agencies for specific casework. This is because there is a large gap between the needs of Forensic Handwriting Examiners (FHEs) and the existing methods of the Pattern Recognition (PR) community[i] The underlying issue is that most of the state-of-the-art signature analysis systems cannot be directly applied to forensic cases as these systems only consider that a questioned signature can be either genuine or forged, and we will argue that forensic analysis requires more in terms of the signatures modalities.

The main objective of this chapter is to highlight the importance of another signature category, namely the disguised signatures, which was largely forgotten by PR-researchers despite of its importance in forensic casework. Furthermore, we present various local features based approaches which we have found suitable for forensic signature verification (involving disguised signatures) during the course of our research.

The rest of this chapter is organized as follows. First of all, Section **2** defines and explains disguised signatures thereby providing the reader with a view of how FHEs approach the signature verification problem. Then, Section **3** covers some of the important related work. Section **4** explains the three local features based off-line signature verification systems explained in this chapter. Section **5** presents the dataset, reports, and debates on the experimental results. Finally, Section **6** concludes this chapter and provides some ideas for the future.

2. Disguised Signatures

In many recent works signature verification has been considered as a two-class pattern classification problem.[8] Here an automated system has to decide whether or not a given signature belongs to a referenced authentic author. If the system could not find enough evidence of a forgery from the questioned signature feature vector, it simply considers the signature as genuine belonging to the referenced authentic author, otherwise it declares the signature as forged.

Apart from the above mentioned two class classification paradigm, another important genre of signatures, especially for FHEs, is the disguised signatures. A disguised signature is written originally by an authentic author but with the purpose of later denial. Here an authentic author tries to disguise his/her signatures to make them look like a forgery. The purpose of conducting a forensic comparison of signatures, therefore, is to consider disguised signatures as well, i.e., all of the following hypotheses have to be taken into account (we note only the types relevant to the discussion at hand):

- The questioned signature is genuine, i.e., naturally written by the writer of the sample signatures (authentic/specimen writer),
- The questioned signature is not genuine and is a product of simulation (forgery) behavior by a writer other than the authentic/specimen writer,
- The questioned signature is unnaturally written and is the product of disguise behavior by the specimen writer, i.e., the specimen writer tried to imitate a forgery attempt of someone else.

A disguised signature differs from genuine signatures with respect to the author's intent when it is written. A genuine signature is written by an author with the intention of being positively identified by some automated system or by an FHE. A disguised signature, on the other hand, is written by the genuine author with the intention of denial, that

Fig. 1. Some example signatures illustrating the different signing behaviors. (Top left, (a)) Genuine signatures of an author, (Top right, (b)) Forged by a skilled forger, (Bottom, (c) and (d)) Disguised signatures by the same original author.

(s) he has written that particular signature, later. The purpose of making disguised signatures can be hundreds, e.g., a person trying to withdraw money from his/her own bank account via signatures on bank checks and trying to deny the signatures after some time, or even making a false copy of his/her will etc. Potentially whatever the reason is, disguised signatures appear in the real world and FHEs face them.[9] Fig. 1 shows some example signatures. Fig. 1(a) shows the genuine signatures of a person and Fig. 1(b) shows a forgery attempt for the same signatures. Here even with the naked eye (FHEs have the additional possibility to view the signatures under various optical devices etc.) the symptoms of a forgery, like hesitation, feedback, and uneven ink spills are visible. Fig. 1(c) and (d) show two disguised attempts by the original author. The signatures in Fig. 1(d) appear more close to the forged signatures (to Fig. 1(b)) as compared to the genuine signatures (to Fig 1(a)). Such disguised attempts thus pose problems in classification.[9]

While disguised signatures were at least mentioned in the last century[1] they do not play a noticeable role in the more recent PR works.[8] Note that, however unlike disguised signatures, disguised handwriting is previously considered in PR studies.[10] The category of disguised signatures has been addressed during the ICFHR 4NsigComp 2010.[11] This was the first attempt to include disguised signatures into a signature verification competition. The systems had to decide whether the author wrote a signature in a natural way, with an intention of a disguise, or whether it has been forged by another writer.

In this chapter we investigate three local features based methods on the publicly available 4NSigComp2010 signature verification competition data set containing disguised signatures. The first system is a combination of scale-invariant Speeded Up Robust Features (SURF) and Fast Retina Keypoints (FREAK). The second system is based on a combination of Features from Accelerated Segment Test (FAST) and FREAK and the third system is based on nine local features with Gaussian Mixture Models (GMMs) classification.

3. Related Work

Signature verification has remained an active field for the last few decades. The state-of-the-art of signature verification from late 1980's to 2000 are presented in Ref. 1 and Ref. 12 Later methods have been summarized in Ref. 8.

Throughout these years, various classification methods based on global and/or local features have been presented. A majority of these methods have been tested for detection of genuine and forged signatures but disguised signatures are generally neglected apart from some initial research,[9] and in some comparative studies of local and global feature based methods.[13] Noteworthy, disguised handwriting in general (classification of disguise versus genuine handwriting only) has been considered.[10] In this chapter we will only focus on related work on using local descriptors for feature computation. For a detailed summary of related work, refer to Ref. 8.

Recently, a local feature based method, Scale Invariant Feature Transform (SIFT), has been introduced to the domain of handwriting[14] and is applied to writer retrieval and identification.[15] Some improvements in the basic SIFT descriptor have also been suggested for character recognition.[16,17] Similarly another local feature based method, Speeded Up Robust Features (SURF), has been used for object and character recognition.[18–20] Furthermore, some local keypoint detectors, e.g., Features from Accelerated Segment Test (FAST), have been used for problems like multiple object tracking,[21] object recognition for smart phone platforms,[22] and recognition of degraded handwritten characters.[23]

All of the above mentioned tasks (including writer/signature identification and retrieval) differ from signature verification in their essence. Therefore, in this chapter, local features and their suitability for signature verification is discussed. Note that some local feature based systems for off-line and on-line signature verification, like Ref. 24 and Ref. 25, have been presented in the past. These systems, however, have not considered disguised signatures which are important for forensic casework. Thus, disguised signatures are explicitly focused on in this chapter.

4. Local Features Based Systems

In this section we provide a short description of the three local features based off-line signature verification systems considered in this study. For the first two systems (SURF-FREAK and FAST-FREAK) we followed the same methodology of local interest point/areas detection and description. The key difference between the two systems is that in the first system the Speeded Up Robust Features (SURF) are used for detecting the signatures' local areas of interest and in the second system the Features from Accelerated Segment Test (FAST) are used. Later, in both the systems, the Fast Retina Keypoints (FREAK) descriptors are used. The third system utilizes a sliding window to extract local features from signatures. In the following Section **4.1** the methodology followed for the first two systems is explained. Later, in Section **4.2** the third local features based system is described.

4.1. Proposed Systems 1 and 2

The proposed Systems 1 and 2 are based on part-based/local features. To perform part-based analysis, it is first required to extract keypoints/ areas of interest from the signature images. The regions around these keypoints are then described using different descriptors.

The proposed System 1 uses SURF keypoint detector and FREAK descriptor. SURF represents an image/signature as a set of keypoints.

SURF is a robust, translation, rotation, and scale invariant representation method. It is partially inspired by SIFT. SURF detects blob like structures from images and uses integral images to compute Hessian matrix. Like other part based approaches, SURF extracts keypoints/ points of interest from parts of image (which represent local features) where the determinant of Hessian is maximum, thus bringing robustness against different variations in the image.[18,19] For further details about SURF, refer to Ref. 20

Once the keypoints are detected, descriptor for each of the keypoints is computed using the recently proposed part based descriptor, FREAK.[26] FREAK is a binary keypoint descriptor inspired by the retina in human visual system. These features are efficiently computed by sampling area around the keypoint on retinal pattern and encoding it as a binary string by comparing image intensities over this pattern. FREAK features are computationally very efficient in comparison to the well-known part-based descriptors, i.e., SIFT[27] and SURF.[20] As the descriptors extracted using FREAK are binary, therefore Hamming distance is used for comparison of descriptors of query and reference signatures. The use of Hamming distance in-turn makes it computationally more efficient as it can be computed using a simple XOR operation on bit level. For further details about FREAK, refer to the Ref. 26.

The proposed System 2 uses FAST[28] keypoint detector and FREAK descriptor. FAST keypoint detector is computationally efficient in comparison to the well-known keypoint detection methods, e.g., SIFT,[27] Harris,[29] and SURF.[20] In addition, FAST gives a strong response on edges, which makes it suitable for the task of signature verification. FAST detects keypoints by examining a circle of 16 pixels surrounding any pixel 'p'. A keypoint is detected at 'p' if the intensities of at least 12 contiguous pixels around 'p' are all above or all below the intensity of 'p' by some threshold 't'. For further details about FAST, refer to Ref. 28. After the detection of keypoints by FAST, System 2 also uses the FREAK descriptor similar to System 1.

The overall process for categorizing a signature started with binarization. We preferred using OTSU[30] binarization since it is computationally efficient and fairly suitable for high resolution signature images as were available in our dataset. After binarization, we applied the SURF/FAST keypoint detector on all the reference signatures, separately, to get the local areas of interest from these signatures. Then, obtained the descriptors of all of these keypoints present in all reference images using the FREAK keypoint descriptor.

All of the keypoints and their associated descriptors describing important local information are added into a database. This resulted in a database-of-features, which contained features for all of the keypoints which were collected from all reference signature images of an author. Once the database-of-features was created, keypoints and descriptors are extracted for the query/questioned signature. Now a comparison was made between the query signature keypoints and the keypoints present in the database-of-features for that particular author.

The same process of detecting local areas of interest using SURF/FAST and then descriptors by FREAK is applied to the query image. After that each of the query keypoints was compared with the keypoints present in the database-of-features. This process continued until all the query signature's keypoints were traversed. Finally, the average was calculated by considering the total number of query keypoints and the query keypoints matched with the database-of-features. This represents the average local features of the questioned signature that were present in the database-of-features of that author. Fig. 2(a) shows an example reference (genuine) signature and Fig. 2(b) shows the corresponding SURF-keypoints extracted from this reference (genuine) signature. Similarly Fig. 2(c) shows a questioned (forged) signature and Fig. 2(d) shows a questioned (disguised) signature, respectively, with SURF-keypoints extracted. Here blue dots represent the original questioned keypoints and red dots represent the keypoints matching with the reference signature keypoints.

For classification, if the average was greater than an empirically found threshold 'α', (meaning, most of the questioned signature local features are matched with reference local features of the authentic author), the questioned signature was classified as belonging to the authentic author, otherwise (meaning, there were only a few query keypoints for whom any match is found), the query signature did not belong to the authentic author.

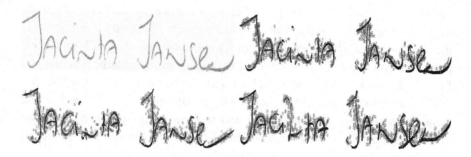

Fig. 2. Some example signatures and extracted keypoints. (Top left, (a)) A genuine reference signature, (Top right, (b)) Keypoints extracted from the genuine reference signature, (Bottom left, (c)) Keypoints extracted from a questioned forged signature, and (Bottom right, (d)) Keypoints extracted from a questioned disguised signature (red = matching, blue = non-matching with the questioned signatures keypoints).

4.2. Proposed System 3

Given a scanned image as an input, OTSU binarization is performed. Then, the image is normalized with respect to skew, writing width and baseline location. Normalization of the baseline location means that the body of the text line (the part which is located between the upper and the lower baselines), the ascender part (located above the upper baseline), and the descender part (below the lower baseline) is vertically scaled to a predefined size each. Writing width normalization is performed by a horizontal scaling operation, and its purpose is to scale the characters so that they have a predefined average width.

To extract the feature vectors from the normalized images, more details in Ref. 31, a sliding window approach is used. The width of the window is generally one pixel and nine geometrical features are computed at each window position. Thus an input text line is converted into a sequence of feature vectors in a 9-dimensional feature space. The nine features correspond to the following geometric quantities. The first three features are concerned with the overall distribution of the pixels in the sliding window. These are the average gray value of the pixels in the window, the center of gravity, and the second order moment in vertical direction. In addition to these global features, six local features describing specific points in the sliding window are used. These include the locations of the uppermost and lowermost black pixel and their positions and gradients, determined by using the neighboring windows. Feature number seven is the black to white transitions present within the entire window. Feature number eight is the number of black-white transitions between the uppermost and the lowermost pixel in an image column. Finally, the proportion of black pixels to the number of pixels between uppermost and lowermost pixels is used.[32]

The Gaussian Mixture Models[33] have been used to model the handwriting of each person. More specifically, the distribution of feature vectors extracted from a person's handwriting is modeled by a Gaussian mixture density. For a D-dimensional feature vector denoted as x, the mixture density for a given writer (with the corresponding model 'A') is defined as:

$$p(x|A) = \sum_{i=1}^{m} w_i p_i(x) \tag{1}$$

In other words, the density is a weighted linear combination of 'M' uni-modal Gaussian densities, 'p_i', each parameterized by a 'D * 1' mean vector, and 'D * D' covariance matrix.[31,34]

5. Evaluation

This section will summarize the experiments which were performed on a publicly available datasat and compared the performance of the three proposed systems with the participants of the 4NSigComp2010 signature verification competition.

5.1. Dataset

The test set of the 4NSigComp2010 signature verification competition is used for evaluation. The collection contains only off-line signature samples. The signatures were collected by forensic handwriting examiners and scanned at '600' dpi resolution. The collection contains '125' signatures. There are '25' reference signatures by the same writer and '100' questioned signatures by various writers. The '100' questioned signatures comprise '3' genuine signatures written by the reference writer in her/his normal signature style and '7' disguised signatures written by the reference writer (who provided a set of signatures over a five day period); and '90' simulated signatures (written by '34' forgers freehand copying the signature characteristics of the reference writer. The forgers were volunteers and were either lay persons or calligraphers.). All writings were made using the same make of ball-point pen and using the same make of paper.

5.2. Results

As mentioned above, the evaluation data contained '3' genuine, '7' disguised, and '90' forged signatures. The unequal proportion of the classes is not problematic as we mainly consider the Equal Error Rates, i.e., when the False Reject Rate (rate at which genuine and/or disguised signatures are misclassified as forged by a system) is same as the False Accept Rate (rate at which forged signatures are misclassified as genuine by a system). We performed all the tests at a machine with the following specifications.

- Processor: Intel Dual Core 1.73 GHz,
- Memory: 1GB,
- OS: WinXP Professional.

We evaluated the efficiency and EER of the three systems explained above and also compared their performance against all the other participants of the 4NSigComp2010 signature verification competition. The participants were tested on the same data under the same conditions and using the same evaluation protocol where only the best performance of the participating systems is reported. This is in accordance with the 4NSigComp2010.[11]

The results of experiments are provided in Table 1. As shown in the table, all of the proposed systems outperformed all the participants of the 4NSigComp2010 signature verification competition in terms of EER. The best system from the competition could achieve an EER of 55%, whereas, the proposed System 3 reached an EER of 20% and both the proposed Systems 1 and 2 have achieved an EER of 30%.

Furthermore, Table 1 also presents the performance comparison of the said systems on the basis of time. The time is given in seconds and is actually the average time taken by any algorithm to report its result on the authenticity of one questioned signature. Two of the proposed Systems, 1 and 2, again outperformed all the participants, especially the proposed System 2 is extremely time efficient.

A general drawback of most of the local features based approaches is the large amount of time they take to compute results. In our experiments, most of the participating systems were relying on global features except the proposed systems, yet the execution of the proposed systems was fairly time efficient when compared to the other systems. This shows that, if utilized properly, local feature approaches show the potential of improving both performance and efficiency of classification.

Table 1. Summary of the comparisons performed among the participants of the 4NSigComp2010 and the proposed local features based systems.

System	Percentage			Seconds
	FAR	FRR	EER	Time
Participant 1	1.1	90	80	312
Participant 2	41.1	90	58	1944
Participant 3	20	70	70	85
Participant 4	0	80	70	19
Participant 5	13.3	80	55	45
Participant 6	87	10	60	730
Participant 7	1.1	80	70	65
Proposed 1	30	30	30	12
Proposed 2	30	30	30	**0.6**
Proposed 3	20	20	**20**	100

Note: Time in seconds (rounded off).

6. Conclusions and Future Work

Forensic signature verification involves various signing behaviors, such as disguised signatures, which are often not considered in the PR research. Therefore, this chapter draws the attention towards disguised signatures and presents a novel evaluation of three of our part based forensic signature verification systems with each other and also with all the systems that participated in the 4NSigComp2010 signature verification competition. We explicitly considered the time required and equal error rate achieved by each system. The three proposed systems are based on SURF-FREAK, FAST-FREAK, and sliding window features.

All of the three proposed systems outperformed the participants of the 4NSigComp2010 signature verification competition by achieving EERs of 30%, 30%, and 20%, respectively. Whereas the EER of the best participating system in the 4NSigComp2010 competition was 55%. Furthermore, on efficiency comparison the proposed local features based systems again performed very well. The proposed System 2 in particular outperformed all the systems remarkably.

In the future we plan to refine our local features approaches as well as test them on much larger and diverse datasets (though we first need to collect such datasets in the future). We also plan to include signature samples written in different languages and analyze the systems capability to classify disguised, genuine, and forged signatures at the same time. We plan to report results in likelihood ratios according to the Bayesian approach, which will make these systems even more useful in the real world forensic casework. This, however, is a difficult task since respective likelihood computation of multiple classes is required in this case.

Acknowledgments

We would like to acknowledge the various forensic handwriting examiners from the Netherlands Forensic Institute who have helped us throughout the course of the studies presented in this chapter. In particular, we are thankful to Dr. Bryan Found, chief forensic scientist Victoria police Australia, and Prof. Charles Berger from Netherlands Forensic Institute.

References

1. R. Plamondon and G. Lorette. 'Automatic signature verification and Writer Identification: the state of the art', in *Pattern Recognition*, vol. 22, pp. 107–131, (1989).
2. F. Leclerc and R. Plamondon, 'Automatic signature verification: the state of the art 1989–1993. *World Scientific, Singapore,* (1994).
3. O. Hilton, 'Can the forger be identified from his handwriting?' in *The Journal of Criminal Law, Criminology, and Police Science*. 43, 547–555, (1952).
4. M. I. Malik, M. Liwicki, A. Dengel, and B. Found, 'Man vs. machine: A comparative analysis for forensic signature verification', in *IGS*, pp. 9–13, (2013).
5. S. N. Srihari, B. Zhang, C. Tomai, S. Lee, Z. Shi, and Y. C. Shin. 'A system for handwriting matching and recognition', in *Symp. on Document Image Understanding Technology*, pp. 67–75, (2003).
6. K. Franke, L. Schomaker, C. Veenhuis, L. Vuurpijl, and I. Erp, M. van Guyon, 'WANDA: A common ground for forensic handwriting examination and writer identification,' *ENFHEX News*. pp. 23–47, (2004).
7. M. Philipp. 'Fakten zu FISH, das forensische informations-system handschriften des bundeskriminalamtes | eine analyse nach ueber 5 jahren wirkbetrieb' Technical report, in *Bundeskriminalamt, Germany,* (1996).
8. D. Impedovo and G. Pirlo, 'Automatic signature verification: The state of the art, in *IEEE Trans. on Systems, Man, and Cybernetics, Part C (Applications and Reviews)* 38, (2008).
9. J. Sita, B. Found, and D. Rogers, 'Forensic handwriting examiners' expertise for signature comparison', in *Journal of Forensic Sciences*. 47, 1117–1124, (2002).
10. C. D. Stefano, A. Marcelli, and M. Rendina, 'Disguising writers identification: an experimental study. in *Int. Graphonomics Society Conference*, pp. 99–102, (2009).
11. M. Liwicki, C. E. van den Heuvel, B. Found, and M. I. Malik, 'Forensic signature verification competition 4nsigcomp2010 — detection of simulated and disguised signatures' in *ICFHR*, pp. 715–720, (2010).
12. R. Plamondon and S. N. Srihari, 'On-line and off-line handwriting recognition: A comprehensive survey', in *IEEE TPAMI*, 22(1), pp. 63–84, (2000).
13. M. I. Malik, M. Liwicki, and A. Dengel, 'Evaluation of local and global features for offline signature verifiation' in *AFHA*, pp. 26–30, (2011).
14. S. Wang, S. Uchida, M. Liwicki, and Y. Feng, 'Part-based methods for handwritten digit recognition', in *Frontiers of Computer Science*, 7(4), pp. 514–525, (2013).
15. S. Fiel and R. Sablatnig, 'Writer retrieval and writer identification using local features' in *DAS*, pp. 145–149, (2012).
16. Z. Zhang, L. Jin, K. Ding, and X. Gao., 'Character-sift: A novel feature for offline handwritten Chinese character recognition' in *ICDAR*, pp. 763–767, (2009).
17. Z. Jin, K. Qi, Y. Zhou, K. Chen, J. Chen, and H. Guan, 'Ssift: An improved SIFT descriptor for Chinese character recognition in complex images' in *CNMT*, pp. 1–5, (2009).
18. W. Song, S. Uchida, and M. Liwicki, 'Comparative study of part-based handwritten character recognition methods' in *ICDAR*, pp. 814–818, (2011).
19. D. Nguyen. Ta, W.-C. Chen, N. Gelfand, and K. Pulli, 'Surftrac: Efficient tracking and continuous object recognition using local feature descriptors' in *CVPR*, (2009).

20. H. Bay, A. Ess, T. Tuytelaars, and L. Van Gool, 'Speeded-up robust features (SURF), Comput. Vis. Image Underst. 110(3), pp. 346–359, (2008).
21. K. Jeong and H. Moon, 'Object detection using fast corner detector based on smartphone platforms', in *ACIS/JNU*, pp. 111–115, (2011).
22. P. Bilinski, F. Bremond, and M. B. Kaaniche, 'Multiple object tracking with occlusions using HoG descriptors and multi resolution images' in *ICDP*, pp. 1–6, (2009).
23. M. Diem and R. Sablatnig, 'Recognition of degraded handwritten characters using local features' in *ICDAR*, pp. 221–225, (2009).
24. S. Pal, S. Chanda, U. Pal, K. Franke, and M. Blumenstein, 'Offline Signature Verification using G-SURF' in ISDA, pp. 586–591, (2012).
25. J. Richiardi and A. Drygajlo, 'Gaussian Mixture Models for on-line signature verification', in ACM SIGMM *workshop on biometrics methods and applications*, pp. 115–122, (2003).
26. R. Ortiz, 'Freak: Fast retina keypoint', in *CVPR*, pp. 510–517, (2012).
27. D. Lowe, 'Object recognition from local scale-invariant features' in *Int. Conf. on Computer Vision*, pp. 1150–1157, (1999).
28. E. Rosten and T. Drummond, 'Fusing points and lines for high performance tracking', in *Int. Conf. on Computer Vision*, pp. 1508–1515, (2005).
29. C. Harris and M. Stephens, 'A combined corner and edge detector' in the 4th Alvey Vision Conf., pp. 147–151, (1988).
30. N. Otsu, 'A Threshold Selection Method from Gray-level Histograms', *IEEE Transactions on Systems, Man and Cybernetics.* 9(1), pp. 62–66, (1979).
31. M. Liwicki, 'Evaluation of novel features and different models for online signature verification in a real-world scenarios' in *IGS*, pp. 22–25, (2009).
32. U.-V. Marti and H. Bunke, 'Using a statistical language model to improve the performance of an HMM-based cursive handwriting recognition systems' in *Hidden Markov Models, World Scientific Publishing* Co., pp. 65–90, (2002).
33. J. Marithoz and S. Bengio, 'A comparative study of adaptation methods for speaker verification, (2002).
34. A. Schlapbach, M. Liwicki, and H. Bunke, 'A writer identification system for online whiteboard data', in *Pattern Recognition*, 41(7), pp. 2381–2397, (2008).

---

[i] An important issue which prohibits the use of PR methods in forensic casework is the output produced by PR methods and its evaluation. More on this issue is presented in a separate chapter by the same authors in this book.

CHAPTER 9

EMERGING ISSUES FOR STATIC HANDWRITTEN SIGNATURE BIOMETRICS

Moises Diaz-Cabrera, Aythami Morales, Miguel A. Ferrer

*IDeTIC. University of Las Palmas de Gran Canaria Campus de Tafira s/n,
E35017, Las Palmas de Gran Canaria, Spain
E-mail: mdiaz@idetic.eu, amorales@gi.ulpgc.es, mferrer@dsc.ulpgc.es*

This paper presents a review of the most recent advances in static/off-line signature recognition using Computer Vision and also identifies some new trends and research opportunities such as the generation of synthetic signatures, time drifting, forger and disguise identification and multilingual scenarios. We conclude that the increasing collaboration between the Pattern Recognition community and Forensic Handwriting Experts will lead to future static handwriting signature milestones.

1. Introduction

Signing is a well-accepted method to authenticate the identity of people and has been carried out for centuries. Law enforcement agencies, governments, financial institutions or forensic units use the signature as identity proof in their daily activities. Traditionally, signature analysis is frequently performed by experienced Forensic Handwriting Experts (FHE). They search for individual characteristics of the owner using common protocols and methods. This analysis is a time consuming task and depends on many factors such as the expert background, available data, and sample quality, among others.

Interest in the development of automatic signature recognition methods from the pattern recognition community began few decades ago. The aim of these systems is to provide a quantitative similarity measure of signatures using an efficient and accurate automatic process. The state-of-the-art of automatic signature recognition is still distant from the results provided by skilled forensics in terms of performance. In fact, there is a large gap between the demands of FHE and the solutions provided by the Pattern Recognition community (PRc). An explanation for this difference is because most of the contributions made by PRc have focused on finding novel methods which outperform previous proposals in terms of quantitative measures, thereby leaving forensic requirements aside.

Several reviews have been published on automatic signature verification, e.g. Plamondon and Shirahi in 2000[1] and Impedovo and Pirlo in 2008.[2] This paper surveys some of the recent advances in automatic signature recognition since then, and identifies emerging trends and new challenges. These areas include: novel feature approaches, available public databases, international competitions, synthetic generation of samples, aging and its influence on signature processing, forger identification, disguised signature detection, and multilingual signature processing, among others.

This chapter is organized as follows: Section 2 surveys the last five years in static signature recognition; Section 3 focuses on the latest performance evaluation developments; Section 4 gathers some current trends and challenges while the conclusions of this paper are discussed in Section 5.

2. State of the Art: Automatic Signature Recognition

Most recent automatic signature recognition developments carried out by PRc are divided among the three main steps of the classical pattern recognition diagram: 1) Signature Preprocessing, 2) Signature Template and 3) Classification.

2.1. *Signature preprocessing*

Signature preprocessing in operative schemes involves signature detection, segmentation and enhancement. Unfortunately, these problems have attracted the attention of only a few researchers. Regarding signature preprocessing, there are three general stages which directly affect the performance of an automatic verification system: find a signature in a document, locate it precisely and extract an accurate image of the signature strokes. Some work has been done in this subject[3] with the Tobacco800 database.

The sheet used for the signature and its influence is another aspect that has scarcely been taken into account in the literature. Paper texture sometimes hinders the extraction of the inked signature, especially when verifying the signature authorship of ancient manuscripts. Ink type should also be taken into account for the segmentation process: A solid ink is usually more distinguishable than viscous or liquid ink.

Additional segmentation challenges arise when the signature image is blended with text or with official stamps commonly found in government forms, bank checks or thin sheets written on both sides. Some proposals to alleviate this problem have been put forth by Douglas and Peucker using a polygonal approximation algorithm and skeleton junction points to remove the text part on the signature in Ref. 4. Other authors take advantage of nonlinear statics methods.[5] A post processing to smooth the signature strokes has also been proposed, especially when proposed texture features are more sensitive to spurious pixels in the stroke.[6]

2.2. *Feature extraction*

Traditionally, features can be classified as global or local. Another kind of classical feature division is the geometrical signature features, statistical features or pseudo dynamic features. Global parameters mean information of the whole signature and local parameters refers to specific information in parts of the signature. Geometrical information refers to the height and the width of the signature as well as their ratio, the area of the signature or the number of points such as loops, end-points, cross-points, etc. A fusion for probability-based directional transitions features such as signature stroke, angles and arcs are also considered. The statistical features model several signature characteristics according to the averages and probability density functions, e.g., pixel density. Pseudo dynamic parameters estimate dynamic parameters from the static signature, e.g. estimating the pressure from ink intensity or pen speed by the stroke curvature.

In the area of pseudo dynamic features, recent advances have been observed in trying to infer the signature trajectory.[7] A novel proposal involves a statistical feature containing local descriptors and ink deposition information based on well-known texture parameters such as Local Patterns.[6,8] Texture-based descriptors are becoming more and more popular due to their good performance. Moreover, in Ref. 9 the authors propose combining geometrical and pseudo dynamic information with texture descriptors. Concisely, they combine co-occurrence matrices, shape matrices and gray-level intensity, looking for vestiges of the pressure signal with multi-scale verification functions.

Popular robust local features detector such as the Scale Invariant Feature Transform (SIFT) or Speeded Up Robust Features (SURF) has also been applied to static signatures, for instance in Ref. 10. In Ref. 11 the authors use Gabor filter-based features combined with SURF features (G-SURF). Recently, optical flow to estimate local stability among signatures is used in Ref. 12 with promising performances.

2.3 *Classification*

The verifier models work with user signatures' features. It usually gives a score which is used to accept or reject the query signature as belonging to the claimed identity. Usual classifiers in pattern recognition are also used in signature verifications, i.e. K-Nearest neighbours, Neural Networks (NN), Hidden Markov Models (HMM) and Support Vector Machines (SVM) among others are well accepted strategies. Recently, the Alternating Decision Tree (ADT) based on decision nodes and prediction nodes achieved encouraging recognition results.[12] An assembly of the above classifiers usually improves performance.

An issue arises when comparing the verifier procedure with FHE work. In pattern recognition the verifier provides a score from which the decision is taken. Meanwhile a forensic expert gives a Likelihood Ratio (LR) of the prosecutor hypothesis (a certain signature was done by a suspected signer) and the defence trial (a certain signature was done by another different signer). A Bayesian analysis is often the key to get a likelihood ratio. This gap remains open although recent efforts suggest that it will be filled in the next years.

3. Performance Evaluation Problem

Performance evaluation of automatic signature verifiers is an important issue to fully appreciate and determine the real reach of this technology. Performance usually is given in terms of ROC (Receiver Operating Characteristic) or DET (Detection Error Tradeoff) plot, in which the False Rejection Rate (FRR) versus FAR (False Acceptance Rate) is depicted for all possible decision thresholds. Often a single number such as the EER (Equal Error Rate) is given as a simplified measure. These statistical measures are usually worked out with signature databases.

The MCYT and the GPDS databases have become popular for pattern recognition. The MCYT database contains 75 users, 15 genuine signatures and 15 skilled forgeries per user. The GPDS includes 881 users, 24 genuine and 30 imitations per user. More signature databases freely released can be found at Ref. 13–19. These database samples are used for both some of the genuine ones to train the models and the other genuine and the forgeries to evaluate their performance.

Table 1 summarizes some of the recent developments and their evaluation provided by the authors. Clearly it is difficult to compare the quality of the different proposals due to the different evaluation procedures.

One approach to limit this drawback is to conduct several international signature competitions with the purpose of comparing different systems on the same databases and with the same evaluation protocols. Some of them are: The BioSecure Signature Evaluation Campaign 2009[20] and 2011;[21] 4NSigComp 2010[22] and 2012;[23] The SigComp2011[24] and SigWiComp2013.[25]

The major problem of the existing databases and competition is that they only include a few aspects of the real word and fail to reflect complex reality. Therefore the validity of the results obtained in the evaluation is limited. Some aspects are difficult to consider in the reduced databases, and they follow: performance with hundreds of

Table 1. Performances of some novel proposed schemes.

Authors	Technique	Database	Results (%)
K. Tselios, 2011[26]	Directional Transitional Features + SVM	GPDS 300 users	EER: 3.80
Luana Batista et al. 2012[27]	HMM + SVM	BrazilianSV 168 users	AER: 5.46
		GPDS 300 users	FRR with RF: 4.50 FAR with RF: 5.19 FRR with SF: 16.81 FAR with SF: 16.88
M.A. Ferrer et al. 2012[6]	Texture features + SVM	GPDS 800 users	EER with RF: 1.64 EER with SF: 16.85
		MCYT75 users	EER with RF: 1.89 EER with SF: 15.41
S. Pal et al., 2012[11]	Gabor filter + SURF features + SVM	GPDS 50 users	RR: 97.05
G. Pirlo et al. 2013[12]	Optical flow + ADT	GPDS 300 users	EER with SF: 4.0

EER: equal error rate, AER: average error rate, FRR false rejection rate, FAR: false acceptance rate, RF: random forgeries, SF: skilled forgeries and RR: recognition rate.

of users, temporal drift, signer neuronal degeneration and aging effect, multilingua signatures (western, Hindi, Bangla, Japanese, Chinese, etc.), writer pose influence on the signature, pencil, inks and sheet influence, ability to detect disguised samples, etc. Additionally, the free distribution of real database compromises the legal identity of users hampering its distribution.

4. New Trends in Static Signature Recognition

In this paper the new challenges faced by researchers is broken down into five topics.

4.1. *Generation of Synthetic Signatures Samples*

The inclusion of real variability in a signature database requires a costly international cooperation in terms of time and money. A current, apparently effective solution is the synthetic generation of databases. This procedure presents the following advantages: (i) it is effortless to produce (once the generation algorithm has been developed), (ii) there is no size restriction (in terms of subjects and samples per subject) since it is automatically produced from a computer, (iii) it is not subject to legal aspects because it does not comprise the data of any real user, and (iv) it eliminates human mistakes such as labeling the data which bias the performance evaluation of the algorithms.

The generation of a new synthetic handwritten signature has emerged as an attractive alternative for researchers during the last years. In fact several proposals have been published. Firstly, a novel methodology was developed by Galbally et al.[28,29] to generate on-line signatures based on flourish and some isolated characters. Later, a static synthetic signature method is related to,[30] which are based on flourish. A trend in this area is to include the diverse variability of real sceneries in the database.

4.2. *Temporal drifting on automatic signature recognition*

The signature, as a behavioral biometric, is sensible to long-term variations which can be related to multiple session acquisitions,[31] aging[32] or neuromotor degenerations,[33] among others. The main effect of aging in signature processing applications is the degradation of intraclass variability. Hence, distinguishing between genuine and forged signatures is a rather complex.

The literature about the effects of time on static handwritten signature recognition is scarce.[32] However, the evaluation of aging in handwriting can be analyzed to extrapolate conclusions. In Ref. 34, researchers identify seven handwriting factors which are affected by aging: legibility, speed, pen grip, pressure, handwriting movements, styles and error corrections. All these factors influence the way a person sign and therefore the performance of automatic signature processing. Recent works study the relevance of aging in handwriting[35] and dynamic signature[31,32] recognition. Therefore, the development of technologies for static signature recognition adaptable to aging effects is a research line to be explored.

4.3. *Forger identification*

Most automatic signature recognition systems try to answer this question: is this signature made by its real owner? In the case of a forged signature, this classification scheme avoids an obvious second question which is relevant for FHE: who has forged the signature? The identification of forgers is a daily task for skilled forensics. However it has not attracted any noticeable role in the pattern recognition research community. In Ref. 36 the researchers evaluate the probability density function of different recognition systems obtained from the forger's signature, the forged signature and the original owner. Their results establish a baseline but do not allow the forger to be identified. Traditional automatic signature recognition systems are mainly based on the global aspect of the signature and the forensics techniques for forger identification. They are focused on local individual characteristics of the strokes or even the analysis of furrows made by the writing tool on the paper. The development of automatic identification techniques based on these local features and its application to forger identification are open topics.

4.4. *Disguised signature recognition*

When a questioned signature is analyzed by a FHE, the analysis is done under the assumption of two possible hypotheses (see section 2.3). In the defense hypotheses there are two possible scenarios: i) the signature was made by a writer different from the original owner; ii) the signature was made by its original owner but it was disguised. Although FHE have faced this problem for a long time,[37,38] the development of an automatic recognition system of disguised signatures is an open challenge. The inclusion of a disguised signature in performance benchmarks is relatively new. As an example, eleven state-of-the-art systems were evaluated to detect disguised signatures during the last two Forensic signature verification competition 4NSigComp2010 and 4NSigComp2012. The results obtained during the second evaluation[23] clearly outperform the previous ones with EER under 30%. A promising performance based on local descriptors was achieved in Ref. 39 with a similar performance to the winners of 4NSigComp2012. This result encourages exploring deeply the feature approaches based on local information, as is proposed by FHE protocols. Again, this is an open challenge and the inclusion of disguised signatures will be more standard in future experimental benchmarks.

4.5. *Multiscript signature recognition*

The signatures are commonly composed by letters and/or flourish and the letters can be written using different scripts. Despite the large number of works dealing with the script-based text recognition and the static signature recognition, most of them study the isolate problem.[40] Some open questions related to multiscript scenarios are: What is the influence of the script in the recognition accuracy? The performance of a system proposed for the script A will be the same for the script B? In Ref. 41, Bangla, Devanagari and Roman script signatures were evaluated by using signature recognition systems. The most common errors occur with the misclassification of Hindi and Devanagari signatures. The signature is a behavioral biometric trait and it can be influenced by cultural aspects. The analysis of the influence of multiethnic characteristics in the signature identification systems is another unexplored topic for automatic signature recognition systems.

5. Conclusions

In terms of performance, state-of-the-art automatic signature recognition seems to be stopped in a performance around EER = 9% if the signature model is trained with genuine and tested with forgeries using the actual databases. Obviously, results vary depending on the database and the forger ability. In search of improvements, the pattern recognition research community is moving to the parameters used in FHE evaluations. This migration opens up a new scenario of applications and research opportunities. This paper offers a survey of some of these new issues but nowadays more and more proposals appear to be trying to bridge the Forensics Handwriting Experts demands and the Pattern Recognition community developments.

New acquisition devices, development of commercial applications, cancelable templates, gender and age estimation are some examples of new trends which have not been included in this work but may be important in the coming years.

References

1. R. Plamondon and S. N. Srihari, "On-line and offline handwriting recognition: A comprehensive survey", *IEEE Trans. Pattern Anal. Mach. Intell.*, vol. 22 (1), pp. 63–84 (2000).
2. D. Impedovo, G. Pirlo, "Automatic signature verification: The state of the art", *IEEE Trans. on Systems, Man, and Cybernetics*, vol. 38 (5), pp. 609–635 (2008).
3. Guangyu Zhu, Yefeng Zheng, David Doermann and Stefan Jaeger, "Signature Detection and Matching for Document Image Retrieval", *IEEE Trans. Pattern Anal. Mach. Intell.*, vol. 31 (11), pp. 2015–2031 (2009).
4. R. Mandal, P. P. Roy, and U. Pal, "Signature segmentation from machine printed documents using contextual information", *Int. Journal of pattern recognition and artificial intelligence*, vol. 26 (7), pp. 1–25 (2012).
5. J. Tan, W.-X. Wang, M.-S. Feng, X.-X. Zuo, "A New Approach Based on Ncut Clustering Algorithm for Signature Segmentation", *AASRI Procedia*, vol. 1, pp. 14–20 (2012).
6. M. A. Ferrer, J. F. Vargas, A. Morales and A. D. Ordóñez, "Robustness of Off-line Signature Verification based on Gray Level Feratures", *IEEE Trans. Information Forensics & Security*, vol. 7 (3), pp. 966–977 (2012).
7. V. Nguyen and M. Blumenstein, "Techniques for static handwriting trajectory recovery: a survey", *Proc. of the 9th IAPR Int. Workshop on Document Analysis Systems*, New York, USA, pp. 463–470 (2010).
8. J.F. Vargas, M.A. Ferrer, C.M. Travieso, J.B. Alonso, "Off-line signature verification based on grey level information using texture features", *Pattern Recognition*, vol. 44 (2), pp. 375–385 (2011).
9. Y. Kamihira, W. Ohyama, T. Wakabayashi, F. Kimura, "Improvement of Japanese Signature Verification by Segmentation-Verification", *12th Int. Conf. on Document Analysis and Recognition*, Washington, USA, pp. 379–382 (2013).
10. R. Guest, O. Miguel-Hurtado, "Enhancing static biometric signature verification using Speeded-Up Robust Features," *IEEE International Carnahan Conference on Security Technology*, Boston, USA, pp. 213–217 (2012).
11. S. Pal, S. Chanda, U. Pal, Franke, K.; Blumenstein, M., "Off-line signature verification using G-SURF", *12th Int. Conf. on Intelligent Systems Design and Applications*, Kochi, India, pp. 586–591 (2012).
12. G. Pirlo, D. Impedovo, "Verification of Static Signatures by Optical Flow Analysis", *IEEE Trans. on Human-Machine Systems*, vol. 43 (5), pp. 499–505 (2013).
13. Signature Verification Competition 2004 Database, available at: http://www.cs.ust.hk/svc2004/download.
14. MCYT Online and Offline Signature Database, available at: http://atvs.ii.uam.es/bbdd_EN.
15. Caltech Signature Database, available at: http://www.vision.caltech.edu/mariomu/research.
16. GPDS960signature database, available at: http://www.gpds.ulpgc.es/download.
17. Database from GAVAB research group, available at: http://www.gavab.es/recursos.html#firmas.
18. Biosecure database, available at: http://biosecure.it-sudparis.eu/AB.

19. SID Signature Database, available at: http://www.sage-eniso.org/content/fr/15/sid-signature-data-base.

20. N. Houmani, A. Mayoue, et al., "BioSecure signature evaluation campaign (BSEC'2009): Evaluating online signature algorithms depending on the quality of signatures", *Pattern Recognition*, vol. 45 (3), pp. 993–1003 (2011).

21. N. Houmani, S. Garcia-Salicetti, et al, "BioSecure Signature Evaluation Campaign (ESRA'2011): evaluating systems on quality-based categories of skilled forgeries", *Int. Joint Conf. on Biometrics*, Washington DC, USA, pp. 1–10 (2011).

22. M. Blumenstein, M. A. Ferrer, J. F. Vargas, "The 4NSigComp2010 off-line signature verification competition: Scenario 2", *Int. Conf. on Frontiers in Handwriting Recognition*, Kolkota, India, pp. 721–726 (2010).

23. M. Liwicki, M. I. Malik, et al., "ICFHR 2012 Competition on Automatic Forensic Signature Verification (4NsigComp 2012*)", *Int. Conf. on Frontiers in Handwriting Recognition*, Bari, Italy, pp. 823–828 (2012).

24. M. Liwicki, M. I. Malik, et al., "Signature verification competition for online and offline skilled forgeries (SigComp2011)", *Int. Conf. on Document Analysis and Recognition*, Beijing, China, pp. 1480–1484 (2011).

25. M. I. Malik, M. Liwicki, et al., "Signature Verification and Writer Identification Competitions for On- and Offline Skilled Forgeries (SigWiComp2013)", *Proc. of the 12th Int. Conference on Document Analysis and Recognition*, Washington DC, USA, pp. 1477–1483 (2013).

26. K. Tselios, E.N. Zois, A. Nassiopoulos, G. Economou, "Fusion of directional transitional features for off-line signature verification," *Int. Joint Conf. on Biometrics*, Washington DC, USA, pp. 1–6 (2011).

27. L. Batista, E. Granger, R. Sabourin, Dynamic selection of generative–discriminative ensembles for off-line signature verification, *Pattern Recognition*, vol. 45 (4), pp. 1326–1340 (2012).

28. J.Galbally, R. Plamondon, J. Fierrez and J. Ortega-Garcia, "Synthetic on-line signature generation. Part I: Methodology and algorithms", *Pattern Recognition*, vol. 45, pp. 2610–2621 (2012).

29. J.Galbally, J. Fierrez, J. Ortega-Garcia and R. Plamondon, "Synthetic on-line signature generation. Part II: Experimental validation", *Pattern Recognition*, vol. 45, pp. 2622–2632 (2012).

30. M. A. Ferrer, M. Diaz-Cabrera, A. Morales, "Synthetic off-line signature image generation", *Int. Conf. on Biometrics*, Madrid, Spain, pp. 1–7 (2013).

31. J. Galbally, M. Martinez-Diaz and J. Fierrez, "Aging in Biometrics: An Experimental Analysis on On-Line Signature", *PLOS ONE*, vol. 8 (7), pp. 1–17 (2013).

32. M. Erbilek, M. Farihurst "Framework for managing ageing effects in signature biometrics" *IET Biometrics*, vol. 1, pp. 136–147 (2012).

33. C. O'Reilly, R. Plamondon, "Design of a neuromuscular disorders diagnostic system using human movement analysis", *Proc. Information Science, Signal Processing and their Applications*, Quebec, Canada, pp. 787–792 (2012).

34. N. Drempt, A. McCluskey, N. A. Lannin "A review of factors that influence adult handwriting performance", *Australian Occupational Therapy Journal* vol. 58, pp. 321–328 (2011).

35. M. Faundez-Zanuy, E. Sesa-Nogueras, J. Roure-Alcobe, "On the relevance of aging in handwritten biometric recognition". *IEEE Int. Carnahan Conf. on Security Technology,* Boston, USA, pp. 105–109 (2012).
36. M. A. Ferrer, A. Morales et al. "Is It Possible to Automatically Identify Who Has Forged My Signature?: Approaching to the Identification of a Static Signature Forger". *In Proceedings of 10th IAPR International Workshop on Document Analysis Systems,* Gold Coast, Australia, pp. 175–179 (2012).
37. C. Bird, B. Found, K. Ballantyne, Doug Rogers, "Forensic handwriting examiners' opinions on the process of production of disguised and simulated signatures", *Forensic Science International,* vol. 195 (1–3), pp. 103–107 (2010).
38. M. I. Malik, M. Liwicki and A. Dengel, "Part-Based Automatic System in Comparison to Human Experts for Forensic Signature Verification", *12th Int. Conf. on Document Analysis and Recognition,* Washington DC, USA, pp. 872–876 (2013).
39. M. I. Malik, S. Ahmed, M. Liwicki and A. Dengel, "FREAK for Real Time Forensic Signature Verification", *12th Int.Conf. on Document Analysis and Recognition,* Washington DC, USA, pp. 971–975 (2013).
40. S. Pal, M. Blumenstein and U. Pal, "Non-English and non-Latin signature verification systems: a survey", *Proc. of first Int. Workshop on Automated Forensic Handwriting Analysis,* Washington DC, USA, pp. 1–5 (2011).
41. S. Pal, A. Alireza, U. Pal and M. Blumenstein, "Multi-script off-line signature identification", *12th Int. Conf. on Hybrid Intelligent Systems,* Pune, India, pp. 236–240 (2012).

CHAPTER 10

BIOMETRIC SIGNATURES IN MOBILITY: THE NEED FOR TRANSFORMATION AND THE OPPORTUNITY FOR INNOVATION

Emilio Paterlini

Software Engineering Manager, Accenture
Viale del Tintoretto 200, 00142 Rome, Italy
E-mail: emilio.paterlini@accenture.com

This chapter discusses how the growing demand for paperless processes in enterprise and government is pushing the development and widespread uptake of innovative technologies, with a strong focus on biometric signatures and new consumer devices. Two case studies explain the benefits of using biometric signatures in a business context.

1. Introduction

Many industry processes are traditionally classified "paper-intensive"; businesses print hundreds of documents, and spend a significant amount of time and resources managing the "paper cycle" from printing to storing or archiving.

Organizations in the banking, government, healthcare, insurance, retail, and telecommunications sectors that need documents to be signed in any place — and the ability to record that data in real time — could benefit from adopting a "green", paperless approach.

In the last 10 years, Accenture has assisted many organizations in implementing digital signature solutions. In doing so, these organizations overcame many challenges, in terms of costs, customer indifference, underdeveloped technology, and the impact on existing enterprise systems.

At the same time, new waves of technology are constantly pushing enterprises to renew their structures and practices, offering a host of new opportunities for change. For example, cloud-based web services like software-as-a-service (SaaS) are allowing businesses to transform their order management and sales support systems.

Electronic products are making it easier to access information anywhere and at any time, with tablets and smartphones dominating the scene within business and in everyday life. Together with faster and more powerful networks (like 4G), these devices enhance communications by enabling real-time connectivity and an "always on" presence.

In the field of biometric technology, many government bodies — such as the Italian Government and the U.S. Food and Drug Administration — have started defining regulations and technical standards that allow electronic signatures and biometric devices to be used in corporate practices. Different regulatory interpretations around the world may have slowed the initial pace of this development, but since 2011, definitions have been converging (e.g. D.Lgs 235/2010 in Italy[1]), finally allowing digital signature technology to become a part of enterprise and government procedures.

2. Mobility and Biometric Signatures

Over the last few years, we have seen significant growth in requests for transformation of enterprise business processes, with a strong focus on eliminating paper-based processes.

Entering a biometric signature is a small, mandatory step in validating an individual's identity, but it introduces the need for complex, more secure technology that is designed to be "tamper-proof", even in low-value transactions.

Compared to other electronic signatures (for example, passcodes and Personal Identification Numbers (PINs)), biometric identification is very

---

[1]D.Lgs. 30 Marzo 2005, n. 82 (Codice Dell'Amministrazione Digitale), after the modifications of D.Lgs 30 Dicembre 2010, n. 235.

efficient and has a huge potential to transform business-to-business (B2B) and government processes — especially when we consider how many forms a typical company would have.

Biometric identification is a perfect fit for many financial and banking procedures, such as opening accounts, issuing insurance policies, filling in application forms, and authorizing transactions. It can also help improve the process of signing service agreements and retail sales receipts, and it has the potential to revolutionize the way healthcare providers process prescriptions, and collect and manage patient records.

Across all industries, there is a clear need to reduce the cost of printing and paper handling, and migrate paper records into digital storage. In some sectors, reliance on physical documents has the added effect of limiting the flexibility of pricing and terms and conditions.

It may be that using biometric credentials shaves seconds — or even minutes — off the time it takes to verify identity, over time adding up to a potential saving of days or weeks. In other situations, adopting a digital approach could save weeks of processing time almost instantly.

Situation: 100 percent paper-based

Consider what happens when a sales agent uses a process that requires physical documents to be distributed and collected before a service is activated.

- The central sales organization couriers paper forms to the sales agency or directly to the agent.
- The customer signs a paper contract, which the sales agent collects and returns to the local sales agency.
- The sales agency periodically ships the papers to head office via ordinary mail, perhaps every two or three weeks.
- Once the service provider receives the delivery, it ships the documents to a third-party company to be scanned and archived in digital storage.
- The digital storage provider enters the data into the service provider's systems and — weeks after the customer signed the contract — the service is activated.

Suddenly we can comprehend why some companies suffer such long latency times in end-to-end contract activation (a raw average of two weeks). The result is delayed revenues, complaints, and ultimately a potential loss of customers.

By simply replacing the physical contract in this scenario with a means of instant, online biometric verification — supported by an automated, cloud-based data processing system — the entire process shrinks from weeks to minutes — or even less.

Situation: Physical documents and salesforce automation

Even in more advanced contexts — for example, a sales agency that uses a salesforce automation (SFA) system — the process is still cumbersome and raises several issues.

- The sales agent asks the customer to sign the physical contract in person and gathers any other supporting documents, such as a copy of the contract, one or more forms of identification, and a record of the payment details.
- The sales agent brings the signed contract and other documentation to the sales agency office where a back-office operator manually uploads the data into the SFA system.
- The key account manager within the service provider's head office checks this data against validation rules and identifies any issues (such as missing or incoherent data).
- If everything is correct, the contract is activated. Otherwise the back-office operator at the sales office will manage the issue. The sales agent may even need to revisit the customer to amend or complete the unsatisfactory information.

This process can take more than 10 working days, which is significantly quicker than a completely paper-based process but still not optimal for a company operating in a fast-paced, competitive commercial environment.

Situation: The potential benefits of reaching full speed

A fully automated system could alert the sales agent immediately if some fields (such as signature, date or payment details) were wrong or missing, and the sales agent could collect and reprocess the data on the spot.

Speeding up the contract submission and acquisition process is an important factor in securing customers and revenues — the sooner the contract is activated the sooner the billing starts. This means more clarity around revenues, reduced interest expenses, and lower back-office costs.

From another point of view, accelerating the process could mean increased customer satisfaction and retention, and fewer complaints and bad reviews. Customers want their subscription activated as soon as possible, and many claims arise from delays in service activation, especially in the consumer market.

Safety and quality first

Although speed is a key consideration, security must also be taken into account. Biometric or digital customer management systems — and the partners involved in delivering them — must be certified as fraud-resistant and must comply with all applicable security standards.

On the face of it this may entail higher costs, but in the long term it likely represents a cost savings. Stringent security measures help prevent fraudulent transactions and forgery. Customers — content that their data is being protected — choose to continue the service rather than looking elsewhere. And a stable customer base means less risk to revenues, not to mention a reduction in legal costs incurred in addressing security breaches.

Automated systems may save time compared to paper-based systems, but the quality of data collected is also important. For example, it takes time to identify, interpret, and rectify an unclear or incomplete signature or application form, and faulty data can lead to inconsistencies, errors, and unsatisfied customers. Better-quality data can mean lower activation and back-office costs, and — in the long run — happier customers.

Going "green"

From another point of view, introducing a completely paperless process can deliver other indirect advantage by boosting a company's "green" credentials. By adopting biometric identification technology, we calculate companies could save approximately 70 kilograms of carbon emissions per signer, per year [see table below]. For some companies, eliminating entire paper-based processes could be a significant step towards reducing their carbon footprint and achieving their stated goals of becoming an environmentally friendly organization.

The following case studies provide two examples in two different industries, where companies could deploy similar biometric technologies and systems.

2.1. *A leading services provider* [1]

The sales department of a major services provider needs a system that collects and stores customers' biometric signatures—using smartphones and tablets — to accelerate the process of signing and processing contracts.

The following table shows an estimate of the number of physical documents the organization processes for its business and consumer clients each month.

Estimated Volume	Business	Consumer
Number of documents (monthly average)	60,000	625,000
Number of documents (monthly peak)	120,000	1,250,000
Estimated Number of signatures required	2,000	6,000
Average document size (kilobytes)	320	300

In the organization's Business Sales area alone, the cost of running a paper-based operation is estimated as follows:

- Printing forms on paper: about €0.03 per sheet (at the common market price) or €432,000 per year.
- Total paper management costs (including couriers, overnight shipping, fax, and mail): €20 per delivery, or €600,000 per year.
- Storage, archiving, and scanning costs: €1.10 per document, or about €1.2 million per year, usually paid to a specialized local company. The average market price is lower (€0.63), but this would still add up to a large total over the course of a year.
- Additional costs in the event of lost documents, and subsequent research and reproduction: €30 per document. This factor is significant, as there is no process for definitively tracking documents and attachments throughout the handling process. The estimated total for lost documents is around €90,000 per year.

So at first glance and according to the estimates, the company is expected to pay roughly €2.3 million per year in paper-related costs, or €1.53 per document. By adopting a biometric data solution, the company could completely eliminate this expense.

One of the key targets for this program was accelerating the process of acquiring customer and contract data, which would reduce the relative cost of entering data in the company's legacy systems. The "form rejection ratio" for contracts entered into the new customer relationship management (CRM) system is less than 2 percent on average, achieving an average end-to-end activation time of four hours, with a peak of just minutes.

2.2. *A bank operating in a multi-channel market*[2]

A bank needs to launch an initiative to improve critical retail banking branch processes. The bank's key objective is to become a multi-channel financial services provider with clear, simple prices, and a fresh, modern brand image.

---

[2] Data and assumptions based on a generic business case.

Technically speaking, the initiative is focused on implementing an approved solution that complied with standards for scanning, certification, and electronic storage of documents related to credit applications and collateral.

Moreover, the company wants to evaluate the costs and benefits of using new technologies such as biometric tablets and digital signatures.

Prior to the project, each of the bank's offices produced approximately 100,000 documents per year (around 1,000,000 pages per year). Most of these were forms relating to product subscriptions, insurance policies, credit card activations, financial operations, and customer surveys.

Following the digital signature program, the bank could save an estimated €350,000 per year (net of running costs) — an impressive result considering the complexity of achieving the bank's multi-channel objectives and the volumes, of documents involved.

The digital signature initiative could also improve data quality and the "form rejection" ratio. Before the initiative, it could be assumed that up to 30 percent of the bank's forms were deemed invalid due to missing signatures. Now, with the biometric solution the application checks the presence of those signatures and alerts the customer that they need to sign the document in real time.

3. Recommendations

Depending on organizations and specific customer needs, Accenture generally recommends a vertical, service-based digital signature solution that integrates biometric signature technology with mobile devices, to facilitate paperless salesforce automation, contract acquisition, and data capture.

Ideally, organizations would choose a B2B system based on commercial off-the-shelf biometric technology. The system would reside on a client-server architecture, supporting multiple mobile devices, enabling compliance with relevant regulations in each jurisdiction, and providing a high level of security (via cyphering, cryptography, etc.).

Organizations need an ally that can take full responsibility for designing and implementing the entire solution and process. This includes providing advice; developing and customizing client-side mobile applications and enterprise servers; and integrating the solution with existing CRM platforms and document archival systems.

4. Conclusion

In the last few years, biometric identification has played a significant role in transforming businesses from paper-based to paperless operations.

The promise of cost savings has finally encouraged a strong uptake of digital and biometric signature systems in the B2B market, replacing old paper-based processes.

Electronic invoicing, low-value transactions, and contract activations are examples of situations where digital signatures are already commonplace.

However, biometric service providers need to focus on continuous improvement and research so they can offer truly complete services that combine low costs with reliable security, regulatory compliance, and compatibility with the latest mobile and network technology.

Acknowledgments

This work is primary based on Accenture Mobility research and project experience.

A special thanks to who supported and reviewed the contents of this paper: Sarah C. Jones, Deborah Santiago, Robyn Rahbar, Michele Marrone, Linda Zanella, Gabriele Mutarelli, Filippo Amicone, Massimo Morganti, Massimiliano Nicosia.

References

1. SFA & Paperless : *I vantaggi del Paperless e la firma digitale*, Accenture Mobility Services, 2012.

CHAPTER 11

BIOMETRIC HANDWRITTEN SOLUTION: A WORLD IN A SIGNATURE

Carlo Nava

Security Solution Architect
Hewlett Packard Italiana s.r.l. dep. Technology Service IT Security Consulting
Via G. di Vittorio, 9 – 20063 Cernusco sul Naviglio (MI) Italy
E-mail: {carlo.nava@hp.com}

This paper presents some advances in the application of biometric signature in HP. In particular, the proposal of HP is to provide a biometric signature infrastructure in order to start the process of acquisition of the contracts that are concluded with the end customer in a "paperless" mode. For the purpose, specific technical and legal rules have been addressed in order to offer complete biometric signature infrastructure solutions to be integrated into customer applications.

1. Introduction

What the company "ask" today? The answer is almost loud: Saving! Today all companies in the world are reviewing their structures and processes to reduce operating costs and thereby increase profitability. For many companies, in addition, the reduction of internal costs is critical for survival in a fast and dynamic market where it is not possible to slow the rush toward greater efficiency. Having business processes efficient, leaner, faster and a reduction of management costs will be the key to success in order to consolidate business and achieve greater profitability.

There are two words that ultimately are part of the vocabulary of any company "Datacenter Optimization" and "Paperless", and in Italy this means "Cloud Computing" and "Biometric Signature" solutions. More and more companies are asking to review their business processes in terms of reduction of the printed paper and greater efficiency in the management of customer data and precisely in this context that HP offers a complete end-to-end proposal that has as its focus the adoption of biometric handwritten signature.

The organization of this paper is the following: Section 2 presents a brief history of biometrics. In Section 3 some of the most relevant laws that makes the use of biometric signature possible are discussed. Although the Sections concerns specifically to Italian laws and regulations it is very interesting since at the moment Italy is at the forefront from a legal point of view in the use of biometric signature. Section 3 and 4 present respectively some issues related to paperless management solutions and the HP vision on the application of biometric signature technology. The application fields for biometric signature are highlighted in Section 5. Section 6 presents a real case of HP project in which biometric signature has been used. The conclusion of the paper and some future trends are reported in Section 7.

2. Biometrics History

Biometric history indicates that the science did not originate at a single place. People all over the world were using the basics for mainly identifying individuals from each other. Therefore, the history of biometrics dates back to a long time. Possibly the most primary known instance of biometrics in practice was a form of finger printing being used in China in the 14th century.

The Chinese merchants were stamping children's palm prints and footprints on paper with ink so as to differentiate the young children from one another. This is one of the most primitive known cases of biometrics in use and is still being used today.

Apart from its Chinese genesis, the use of biometrics was also noted elsewhere in the world. Up until the late 1800s, identification largely relied upon "photographic memory". In the 1890s, an anthropologist and police desk clerk in Paris, Alphonse Bertillon, decided to fix the problem of identifying convicted criminals and turned biometrics into a distinct field of study. Bertillon developed a technique of multiple body measurements which later got named after him — Bertillonage. His method was then used by police authorities throughout the world, until it quickly faded when it was discovered that some people shared the same measurements and based on the measurements alone, two people could get treated as one. After the failure of Bertillonage, the police started using finger printing, which was developed by Richard Edward Henry of Scotland Yard, essentially reverting to the same methods used by the Chinese for years. (which still is going strong!).

Biometric history in the recent past (three decades) has seen drastic advancements and the technology has moved from a single method (fingerprinting) to more than ten prudent methods. Companies involved with new methods have grown into the hundreds and continue to improve their methods as the technology available to them also advances. Prices for the hardware required continue to fall making systems more feasible for low and mid-level budgets and thus making this more adaptable in small businesses and even households.

As the industry grows however, so does the public concern over privacy issues. Laws and regulations continue to be drafted and standards are beginning to be developed.[1]

3. Italian Law and Digital Documents

Italy is at the forefront in the use of legal digital signature being the first country to have given full legal effect to electronic documents from 1997 and being the one with more widespread in Europe. Today, the laws governing the digital signature and the preservation of digitally signed documents are manifold, below we give an indication to the reader about the main laws and regulations that driven this complex environment:

3.1. *Reference standard in the field of management, use and validity of electronic documents*

- *DPR 28 december 2000, n. 445 "Consolidated text of the laws and regulations relating to administrative documents".*
- *D.Lgs 7 march 2005, n.82 "Digital Administration Code"*

3.2. *Statement about electronic signatures*

- *Decree of the President of the Republic 7 april 2003, n.137 — Regulation laying down provisions for coordination in the field of electronic signatures in accordance with Article 13 of Legislative Decree 23 January 2002 n. 10.*

• *Decree of the President of the Council of Ministers 22 february 2013. Technical rules for the generation, verification and affixing of advanced electronic signatures, qualified and digital, under articles 20, par. 3, 24, par. 4, 28, par. 3, 32, par. 3, letter b) , 35, par. 2, 36, par. 2, e 71.*

3.3. Legislation on the preservation of electronic document

• *D.P.C.M 13 january 2004 - Technical regulations for the formation, transmission, storage, duplication, reproduction and validation, even temporarily, of documents.*
• *Decree of the President of the Council of Ministers 13 january 2004 Technical regulations for the formation, transmission, storage, duplication, reproduction and validation, even temporarily, of electronic documents (G.U. n. 98 del 27 april 2004).*

3.4. Technical rules

• *Decree of the President of the Council of Ministers 22 february 2013. Technical rules for the generation, verification and affixing of advanced electronic signatures, qualified and digital, under Articles 20, par. 3, 24, par. 4, 28, par. 3, 32, par. 3, letter b), 35, par. 2, 36, par. 2, e 71.*
• *Decree 3 april 2013, n. 55 Regulations on emission, transmission and receipt of electronic invoices to be applied to general public under Article 1, pars. 209 to 213 of the Law of 24 December 2007, n. 244, entered into force June 6, 2013.*

3.5. Privacy data "Guarantor" rules

• *Measure of the Privacy Guarantor n. 37 del 31 january 2013 — Provision of the Privacy Guarantor mode of processing of data relating to the signing of documents with digital signature based on a biometric authentication procedure performed by SignPad ("tablet").*

The Italian Legal Code, distinguishes the concepts of "electronic signature", "advanced electronic signature", "qualified electronic signature" and "digital signature":[2]

Electronic Signature: the set of data in electronic form attached to or logically associated with other electronic data, used as a method of authentication;

Advance Electronic Signature: the set of data in electronic form attached to or associated with an electronic document that allow the identification of the signer of the document and provide the unique connection to the signer, created using means that the signer can maintain exclusive control, linked to the data to which that the signature refers to allow to detect whether the data have been subsequently modified (a biometric signature is a example of Advance Electronic Signature);

Qualified Electronic Signature: a particular type of advanced electronic signature obtained through a procedure which guarantees the unique connection to the petitioner and his unique authentication information, which was created using means that the signer can maintain exclusive control and linked to the data to which it relates in such a way as to allow to detect if the data has been amended, which is based on a qualified certificate and created by a secure device for creating the signature, such as the instrumental apparatus used for the creation of electronic signatures;

Digital Signature: A special type of advanced electronic signature based on a qualified certificate and a system of cryptographic keys, one public and one private, related to each other.

If the reader wonders why of such a long and complex legal discourse is essential to recall that these legal conditions now take the opportunity to create legal documents completely digital. Never before today the technology offered by the market and legal conditions can be met by offering unique opportunities for a future complete digital.

The main stages of the life cycle of the document completely digital can be summarized as follows:

- Generation
- Content Management
- Composition
- Subscription (Signature)
- Conservation and Distribution.

3. Paperless Management

The advantages of paperless management can be summarized in the following items:

- Eliminating the costs of the paper: storage costs and consumables Saving in terms of time-man: for research and consultation of paper archive
- Reducing risk of legal argument: linked to the possible loss of the original document or its non-compliance.
- Efficiency of the entire supply chain contract management: service (less time distribution of the document, better versioning management, greater speed and ease of access by the various departments involved).

This makes it possible the complete management of document flow by biometric signature affixed by the customer. Too often, however, we think this is the main benefit omitting the importance of the management of customer data.

The fully digital process, such as a sale, allows the real-time data of the contract signed, filled and sent to the customer care systems immediately.

4. HP vision for Biometric Signature like Paperless Solution for Legal Contracts

HP, through the Italian Business Innovation Center, analyzed various products able to achieve a valid biometric signature, about many years.

Only in the last two years, there have been technical and legal rules in order to offer at its customers a complete solution of dematerialization from the document production until its storage, HP call this process "dematerialization ab origine", as Figure 1 shows.[3]

It's easy to understand how the component of biometric signature is an important junction in the complete process of dematerialization.

In relation to what stated above the proposal of HP is to provide the company a biometric signature infrastructure in order to start the process

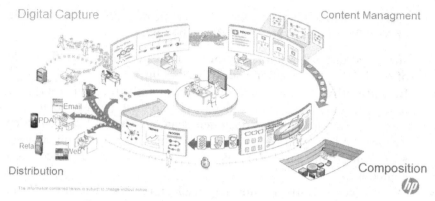

Fig. 1. A schematic illustration about paperless HP vision.

of acquisition of the contracts that are concluded with the end customer in a "paperless" mode. The solution includes:

- the installation and configuration of a "biometric signature software " dedicated to client stations;
- a graphics tablet (signature PAD), which is connected to the USB port of the workstation, through which you can capture the signature of the customer;
- the installation and configuration of an APP on the tablet (Android or IOS) in order to operate in complete mobility.

The process of acquiring the signature of the customer will allow "the safety" of the contract with the creation of a PDF/A in which "shall be applied" the biometric data.

The proposed HP does not have the simple goal of providing an infrastructure for the acquisition of the biometric signature but, in particular, the complex process of analysis of detail necessary to make the flow of documents valid according to the law.

The solution provides strong security features which can be summarized as follows:

- **Protection of biometric data**: once the document has been produced, it is important not to make accessible (modified and/or reusable) biometric data relating to the signature affixed by the signer. For this issue the biometric data are managed in ISO/IEC (19794-7:2007). The parameters thus collected are asymmetrically encrypted using the public key of a certificate with a specific mode of AES 256-bit encryption and RSA 2048 bit;

encrypted using the public key of a certificate with a specific mode of AES 256-bit encryption and RSA 2048 bit;

• **Immutability of the document**: once embedded in encrypted biometric data, a digital signature is applied to the document. The immutability of the document can be checked with Adobe Reader. When you open the PDF file there is immediately a warning, in case the file has been modified since you signed it;

• **Do not re-usability of the acquired signature**: The mechanism used to generate the digital signature inextricably linked to the hardware signature used to sign the document with the sign itself.

Obviously, the solution of HP was developed and designed to meet the requirements of the law, and allow simple inclusion of signature infrastructure within the business processes in use.

Figure 2 shows the technical characteristics of the signature collection through the signature PAD.

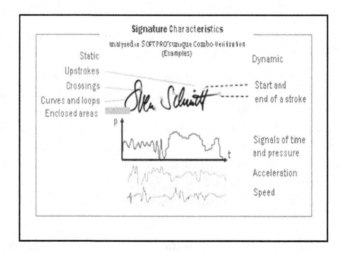

Fig. 2. A schematic illustration about the characteristics of bio-signature.

5. Application Fields for Biometric Signature

As previously described, it is now possible to use biometric signature in a very large number of applications like:

- **Paperless offices**: Biometric signature speeds up document approval processes, authorizations, etc. and allows to sign from anywhere at any time. It eliminates misuse of employee passwords or ID cards and IT department's time associated with password management and ID cards lost. It improves legibility of documents since all of them are filled in using the keyboard. It also produces important savings in paper and printer toner usage, paper documentation archive and management.

- **Fraud protection** in credit card and private label credit card use: While other biometric parameters, PINs and passwords can be obtained without the knowledge and/or consent of their owners, handwritten signature has to be done by the user in the very moment it is required. Then, biometric signature is the safest alternative to reduce credit card theft use and charge backs from stolen or forged cards at the point of sale, banks or in e-commerce applications.

- **Cash management** control for financial departments and cash registers: Paper based transactions and handwritten documents or forms can be manipulated by changing numbers once they have been approved and signed or by forging the initials and/or signatures. Identification numbers and/or passwords to log on cash registers can also be obtained without the owner's consent. Biometric signature can be easily used to reduce or eliminate chances of theft and/or fraud.

- **Time attendance systems** to keep track of employee attendance: Biometric signature has to be made by the employee at the time he/she is entering or leaving the company premises. Therefore, biometric signature based attendance systems help companies to monitor compliance with working hours preventing employees from bad practices like supplanting the identity of others (in card, PIN, password, employee ID based systems), delays, etc.

- **Biometric for Access Control, Privacy and Security**: From a certain perspective, security is broken. The security authorization triangle (possession, knowledge, identity) has in some cases been reduced to a single point (knowledge) because of the limitations to possession attributable to virtualization, and because of the limitations to identity attributable to the use of static biometrics. New technologies in mobile and cloud computing, pattern recognition and user interaction provide a potential path forward an identity-matching ecosystem in which both privacy and security needs can be accommodated.

- **Control Quality and Inspection**: The biometric handwritten solution can be provided to make more efficient the quality control process inside to operative production process. The use of mobile devices (tablet) that allow to recover the biometric signature combine to a dedicate IT infrastructure, can be able to offer a more rapid inspection control quality for the production cycles, and can be sure to identify the inspector. This application can be offered to more company where the quality of the product is critical and the inspection processes are required by law (e.g. pre- and post- flight airplane check).

6. Real Case: Dematerialization Contract for a Telco Company

In this Section a real case is presented concerning an HP project for a Telco company having the aim to dematerialize the telephone contracts that are signed at the point of sale. The infrastructure set consists of a client component installed at the client PC dealer and a component of BackEnd responsible for document management. The design analysis for the project has led to develop a new stream of acquisition of identity documents of the customer. This flow has enabled us to inextricably bind the biometric signature affixed to the contract, evidence of identity of the customer and the contract itself creating a single file PDF/A. At the end of the sales process the contract is digitally encrypted, the original file is sent in real time to a secure storage system and any copy thereof may be sent by mail.

In addition to saving paper, the solution has introduced a new and faster sales process by allowing the availability of contractual data in real time. The system of biometric acquisition and processing of data were endorsed by the Italian authority for the protection of personal data (*Privacy Guarantor*).

Now the Telco company is thinking about to extend the biometric solution also for internal process where is mandatory a sign for complete the document.

7. Conclusion and Future Trends

In this paper some steps towards the inclusion of biometric signature technology into HP customer solutions have been discussed. The future will be more and more digital. New technologies that allow us to live the digital experiences for all the same as those to which we are accustomed, such as sign, are within the reach of companies. The true strength of a solution of biometric signature is in its simplicity of execution, everyone got used to sign since we are young. The technology is also well mature, laws finally complete and indicate directly the legal validity of the solution, therefore, in the next few years we will see the spread of devices capable of capturing the biometric signature. Already today there are smart phones capable of responding to the legal requirements of signature and will not be long, for which it will be possible to sign a contract of insurance directly from the phone, without need to have a pin code or automatic code generation systems.

References

1. A. K. Jain, A. A. Ross, K. Nandakumar, *Introduction to Biometrics*, Stringer, 2011.
2. http://www.digitpa.gov.it/
3. http://www8.hp.com/us/en/business-solutions/index.html

INDEX

system performance, 62
Temporal drifting, 117
Time function based features, 43
updating system knowledge, 53
useful information, 62
WANDA, 73

wavelet approximation, 43
weight, 59
Weighted Majority Vote,
  53
Wrapper, 57
writer dependent, 87

Printed in the United States
By Bookmasters